INTRODUCTION

A white terry cloth towel absorbed most of the blood from her injury. All that escaped the towel's fibers dripped thickly to the waxed hardwood floor making the finish seem dull. The blood seemed minimal compared to the deep head wound that would serve as a reminder of an evening gone wrong.

In Camille's twenty-eight years of living, she had acquired an unconventional habit of collecting tattoos. There were no roses or meaningful symbols of something beautiful. Her tattoos consisted of keloid scars or mental bruises caused by men she loved. Fortunately, none of her abusive relationships had been back to back. Camille had been in some healthy relationships with intelligent, handsome and nice men but without any warning or explanation that she could see, a boyfriend whom she cared very much for would abuse her.

Barely hearing the 911 operator's voice above her own heartbeat, she breathlessly gave the operator her name and address. Camille's thoughts whirled quickly as she began mumbling softly to herself.

"What am I doing wrong? How is it that I always manage to eliminate a good man from my life? What could I have done to avoid this from happening to me?" Feeling faint and the need for more air, despite her fear, Camille opened the door and sat outside and leaned against the coolness of the iron black rails along the stairs.

911 IS FOR EMERGENCIES ONLY

A full moon lit the sky as a warm midnight breeze blew through the window of the patrol car. For police officers like McIntosh and his partner, nights like these were fused with excitement that almost guaranteed an evening of danger.

Beep! Beep! "Three Adam Fifteen, handle a domestic violence call at 4350 Don Carlos Drive. A female is being battered by her boyfriend. Three Adam Fifteen handle code 2 high," the intense female voice broadcasted over the dispatch radio.

Officer McIntosh picked up the radio microphone and acknowledged, Three Adam Fifteen roger!"

"Hell," officer McIntosh shouted as he pounded his fist into the dashboard. Gripping the steering wheel tightly and contorting his face, he blew out a frustrated sigh. "Man! Another domestic violence call. I hate responding to this crap. They're all a big waste of time!"

Turning to his partner, McIntosh slowed the patrol car down to cruise speed and relaxed. "Let's take our time, we're in no hurry to handle this call. Hopefully, by the time we get there, the ignorant broad's boyfriend will be gone. That way, we only have to take a report."

Laughing, his partner responded, "I'm definitely with that! I don't understand why these women get involved with these losers. All they have to do is leave them. I'm sick of this junk too. We could be doing some real police work instead of babysitting. I was hoping to catch somebody tonight."

Through the dark blue of the night, a red neon sign blinked the shape of a burger. Rubbing his stomach, McIntosh suggested, "How about stopping at Burger King first. I'm, starving."

"Sounds good," his partner agreed. "Maybe the boyfriend will have enough time to leave. With our luck he'll probably still be there, lying comfortably on the couch like nothing happened. Just like most of um do."

"We'll have two number ones," McIntosh blurted into the drive-thru speaker. "And super size um!"

Backing the car into a space at the back of the restaurant, the officers tore into the bags and began eating nonchalantly. With a mouth full of fries, McIntosh's partner asked, "I wonder why we get so many domestic violence calls? It doesn't make sense! Men know that if they hit their women they're going to jail. Women know that if their men hit them once, they'll do it again. This crap don't make sense!

"Nothing that has to do with women makes sense," McIntosh replied. I've been a police officer for nine years now and I still don't understand why people do what they do. All I know is that I don't want to get married and end up unhappy like the people we serve. Seeing what I have on this job has made me afraid to get married."

"Three Adam Fifteen come in..." McIntosh picked up the microphone and responded, "Three Adam Fifteen go..."

"Three Adam Fifteen the victim from your call has called a second time. She stated that you are still needed. Three Adam Fifteen what is your E.T.A. to the location?"

McIntosh looked to his partner for an explanation. "Three Adam Fifteen we have a ten minute E.T.A. We are responding from the other end of the division."

Laughter tumbled out of the windows of the patrol car as the officers glanced at each other and then took another bite out of their burgers. Ten minutes later, they tossed their trash out the window and sped out of the parking lot.

"Remember the time we responded to that domestic violence call on Hoover and 25th Street? McIntosh asked his partner.

"I think so. Are you talking about the one where that Mexican punched his wife in the mouth and knocked out her front teeth?

"Yeah, that's the one!"

The officers reminisced about the call. They recalled how shocking it was to see the suspect casually open the front door as if nothing had taken place.

"Did you call the police?" the officers asked. The husband calmly told them his wife called because he punched her in the mouth. His explanation was, "she was talking too much." With a strong Spanish accent, he stated, "I just punch her once. It's okay. No problem." What the officer found more shocking was that the husband couldn't understand why he was being arrested.

"Why do Mexicans think that they can hit their wives anytime they want?" asked McIntosh.

"What about white boys who make a little money?" responded his partner. "They think they're above the law. What is it they always say?"

"I pay more money in taxes than you make a year! McIntosh answered in a sarcastic high pitched voice. "Screw em, Screw everybody, I'm sick of this. It never ends!"

Turning onto Don Carlos Drive, McIntosh thought out loud, "There's something familiar about this address. I think I've been here for something before."

"Well, we should know for sure in a few minutes. I believe that's our victim sitting pathetically on those steps up ahead."

"I hope she's not like most of the stupid women who are always calling the police and insisting we arrest their old man for hitting them."

"Yeah, and then the next day they always come down to the station and drop the charges. I can't believe this. This is our third domestic violence call and we've only been out of roll call for an hour and a half!"

WHY ME?

Frame this picture of me
neck swollen from tight fingers/ hot palms
Frame this picture of me
and watch as my eyes change colors with the
appearance of angels

I know that I am divine
and I pray that my life
was a Celebration to the disenfranchised
And an oracle to fragments of rock
blessed with the power to be crystal
and filled with the Holy Spirit of comets
and I pray that my death
be a Celebration... a quiet repast of joy
on the lips of leftover loved ones let the story be
re-told

Rhonda L. Mitchell

Camille rushed to the phone between patients to answer the call that had been holding for her at least ten minutes. Because of her hectic workload earlier that morning, she had neglected to answer the first time someone had called.

"I think it's the same guy who called earlier," one of her co-workers told her. "He's been holding for a while."

She picked up the receiver in her friendly and professional voice. "Hello, this is Camille."

The caller was an ex-boyfriend who asked Camille if he could come over about eight that evening for a casual visit. Since she wasn't doing anything after work. Camille agreed to let him come. She hadn't seen him in a while and was actually starting to miss him.

After a monstrous work load and demanding patients driving Camille up the wall all day, she wanted nothing more than to go home, soak in the tub and pour herself a glass of wine.

Sitting on the 10 freeway in rush hour traffic frustrated, she scanned through the FM stations. Country music was to depressing. R&B and easy listening were too soft. Rock and Roll was out of the question. And then there was rap! The last thing

Camille needed was to sit in traffic moving two miles an hour and listening to socially dysfunctional gangster talk about shooting people.

One hour and fifteen minutes later, she arrived to the safe haven of her home. Normally, she was a tidy person but on this day, she immediately kicked off her shoes and disrobed her clothing without closing her blinds. Camille's baby toe pulsated when she removed her tight fitting pumps. "Damn, I've got a run in my fifteen dollar Givenchy stockings," she cursed. "Now, all I need is to get my bath going and the night will be alright." Camille grabbed a wineglass off the bar as she passed through her tastefully decorated living room.

Camille slipped deeper in the Estee Lauder bubble bath she had run with almost scorching water. Steam seeped through the door and fogged up her vanity mirrors in the candle light reflections. Sipping on a glass of white wine, the day's stress melted off of her and out of her memory.

As she stood in the mirror gently rubbing lotion on her body, Camille scrutinized her appearance. Except for the dark circles under her eyes which weren't permanent yet, she still looked pretty good. There were only the occasional pimples that she figured came from taking birth control pills, stress or not drinking enough water. The tattoo reminders seemed to be invisible to her eye, though they might have been visible to anyone else.

Camille slipped on a thin blue checkered flannel robe that she received from a boyfriend two Christmases before. The thought of the robe caused her to reminisce on her disappointment. She had wanted a ring, not the cheap, flimsy robe she got.

Striking a wooden match against her fireplace, Camille lit a lavender candle and placed it carefully on the carved end table near the crystal stemmed glass of Chablis she had poured herself. Stepping over the shoes and clothing still lying on the floor from her return home, she melted into the down of her sienna colored love seat. She had drifted off somewhere between tranquility and music when she was awakened by a thundering which seemed to be coming from the front of the house.

Coming back from her haze, Camille realized that the thunder was actually knocking at the front door with hisses of profanity coming from her friend.

Arriving sometime after 8 o'clock, Camille's friend peered though the crack of the blinds trying to catch an image of what he was sure was the flicker of candlelight. He had already pressed the doorbell twice and tapped a few times. The longer he waited the angrier he became. His thoughts and paranoia began to enrage him more as he believed he had seen stockings and a dress strewn on the floor through the edge of the blinds. He walked back to the front porch and began banging on the door. He even kicked it a couple of times as he voiced his frustration.

"That stupid tramp," he said under his breath. "She knew I was coming over. Why the hell didn't she tell me that she was going to be screwing around with somebody? She did this on purpose. Tramps are always playing games!"

Hearing a soft rustle at the door, her friend listened intently.

"Who is it?" Camille asked softly.

"Who in the hell do you think it is? It's me."

"Who is me?" Camille sounded puzzled.

"Who do you think Camille?"

"Oh my God!" Camille thought out loud, removing the chain and quickly opening the door to let him in. "I'm sorry, I forgot you were coming by."

"How in the hell could you forget. I called you at work to tell you I was coming by."

"I'm sorry," Camille apologized again. "I had a rough day."

"Yeah right, if you were gonna have company tonight then you should have told me and I wouldn't have come," he said with rage in his voice.

Camille was surprised by his comments. She realized she didn't have to prove anything to him anymore yet somehow felt compelled to show him he was wrong.

"Company? What company?" she asked. "There's nobody here! Come in and take a look for yourself."

"I don't want to look around. I'm leaving," he told her.

"You don't have to leave. Come in."

He then brushed Camille aside and forcefully walked through the door. With an intense look on his face, he checked around the immediate area of the apartment for any visible signs of a man's presence. A loosely knitted Afghan was lying on the living room floor just as it had many times before when they made passionate love. Camille had made it by hand out of a velvet black yarn especially for those times. But mostly, she disliked the stinging sensation of rug burns. The memory brought a small smile to her friend's lips, but for only a brief second.

Focusing his attention on the two wineglasses sitting on the coffee table, he asked, "If nobody's here then why are there two glasses on the table?" Camille laughed joyfully. Her ex-boyfriend wasn't at all amused. As she continued to laugh, his left eye twitched and a cold, angry look flashed across his face. Camille had seen this look many times just before, usually right before he would break out into a rage.

"Why are you jealous?" Camille asked with a smirk. "There's nobody here. There are two glasses on the table because one of them was cracked so I got another one. Even if there was another man here, so what? You're not my man anymore. I can do whatever I want!"

By now, his cheeks were pulsating with anger. He took another look around the room to verify Camille's statement. He wanted to make sure no one else was in the house. Pointing his finger in her face, he began to shout.

"You think this is funny don't you? Why are you always trying to play games with me?" he asked.

Camille tried to physically stop him by grabbing his arm.

"What are you talking about? I'm not playing games!" she responded.

He turned away from her with the purpose of getting her attention knowing she would try to stop him from leaving. This time, things were different. For some reason he didn't submit to her actions.

Suddenly, with all of his strength, he balled his fist and launched an overhand right in Camille's face. The first punch exploded on her lips. The force of the blow caused her body to jerk and then sway before collapsing on to the floor.

It seemed like a bad dream in slow motion. Camille opened her mouth to scream but only a strained silence seemed to escape. "Oh my God!" she thought to herself. "This is it. He is finally going to kill me."

"It's not so funny now is it?" he screamed.

Dazed and terrified, she scrambled on her knees and made a desperate reach for the phone.

"Where in the hell do you think you're going?"

Her ex-lover quickly intercepted her attempt to brace herself by delivering a swift kick to her face. Blood squirt from her nose and mouth. Trying to dodge the next kick, she shifted her body sideways. Her failed effort caused his shoe to graze her forehead. Camille felt herself losing consciousness.

Although never this serious, Camille had made it through this too many times in the past for her to give up and die now.

"I can't die! I've got to hang on!" she said to herself.

Again, she made a futile grab at the phone sitting on the coffee table. "Tramp! Do you want the phone so you can call the police? Huh? If you want the phone then I'll give you the damn phone!" he shouted down at her.

With all the force of an angry man, he picked up the telephone and hurled it down on top of her head. A long gash opened up on the top of her head. Camille's appearance grew hideous. Blood poured from her head and mucus hung from underneath her nostrils.

She sat on the floor with blurred vision, slumped over and delirious. Her ex-boyfriend's enraged face faded into nothing more than a dark shadow leering down at her. She couldn't make out what he was doing to her but every few seconds she felt a sharp pain stab her in her ribs. Uncertain of how much time had passed, she finally saw the ghostly figure of her ex-boyfriend turn around and disappear out of the apartment.

Camille's face throbbed and hurt like hell. She had never been a very religious person but she desperately pleaded to God.

"Please Lord, don't let me die!"

For a brief moment, Camille thought she had died. She saw herself traveling through a tunnel toward a soft light. Realizing the light was actually the flame of her lavender candle, she realized she was still alive.

Her body must have been in shock because her legs and arms wouldn't respond when she wanted to stand up. The only thing she could manage to do at that moment was to cry and rock her head from side to side. She continued to rock until she regained full consciousness.

It seemed like an hour to Camille before she could gather enough strength in her legs to walk into the bathroom and splash cold water across her face. Peering though blurred vision in the mirror above the sink she began to shake all over again. The hideous sight of the face she thought only hours ago to be attractive, terrified her more than the beating had. At least it had ended, she saw the damage in the mirror as endless torture. Her tears burned like a thousand bee stings as they rolled down her face across the bruises and gashes protruding from her cheekbones and lips. Brushing her hair back and dabbing cautiously at her face, she painfully wiped away as much of the ugly reminder as she could.

Reflecting briefly on the evening leading up to the attack, Camille began to experience a rush of mixed emotions. Her thoughts came in and out of focus as the 911 operator repeated the question in the background of the receiver still sticky with Camille's blood.

Camille felt she had screwed up again. Rationalizing, she thought, "Maybe I brought it on myself by laughing at him. But why did I upset him like that? I know there is no excuse for a man to hit a woman. But why did I upset him like that? I know he's sensitive. I shouldn't have taunted him like that. I should have let him go when I knew he wanted to be alone, but I was to busy being flattered by his jealousy."

Still juggling the reasons inside her head, Camille became angrier when she realized that at least 15 minutes had passed and the police still had not arrived. Feeling desperately weak, she dialed 911 again to inquire why.

Waiting for the operator she reflected on the attitude of the police. Thinking, "Do women literally have to take matters into our own hands like Lorena Bobbit before anyone listens? Where are they? If this was life or death, I'd be dead right now!"

"911, operator 27. What are you reporting?" the voice sounded mechanical to Camille.

Clearing her voice, Camille hoarsely said, "this is my second time calling! I called you guys fifteen minutes ago and nobody has shown up yet!"

Sounding removed and unsympathetic, the operator asked, "Where are you calling from ma'am?"

"You know where I'm calling from!" Camille shouted. "My address is on your 911 screen!"

"Ma'am the information on the screen is not always correct. That's why we have to ask you where you are calling from. Are you calling from 4450 Don Carlos Drive?"

"Yes. Is someone coming?

"We have a unit on its way. They should be there shortly," the operator answered.

"We have a unit on its way. They should be there shortly," the operator answered.

"I've been waiting 15 minutes..."

Still calm, the operator concluded, "I'm sorry ma'am. They'll be there as soon as they can. Please don't call back ma'am because it's not going to make us respond any faster."

Camille felt hopeless. There was nothing she could do but sit tight and hope the police would come soon.   "Maybe it's really busy tonight?" she told herself. "They must have a lot of calls to handle."

Fighting back the tears, Camille answered, "I think that I made him mad."

"Okay ma'am. The police will be there soon. Try not to move around and put pressure on any bleeding wounds," the operator calmly added.

Operator #27 could hear the distress in Camille's voice. She sounded as if she were in excruciating physical pain and emotional anguish. But so did the other one hundred and thirty-nine domestic violence victims who had called that day. So what was new? Early in the operator's career, she would have had great concern for a call like Camille's. After five years of dispatching officers to domestic violence calls, one call seemed no more important than the next. The night was young and the 911 line was already backed up. Anyone who dialed 911 had to listen to a tape-recorded message for two minutes before getting through to an operator. The operator was only concerned with getting the necessary information from Camille so that she could relay it to the responding officers.

"If you aren't gonna come then the next time you're gonna have to arrest me cause I'm gonna kill him!" Camille cried.

"Okay ma'am, someone will be there shortly."

"That's what they all say," the operator thought with disgust as she hung up.

Hanging up the phone in frustration, Camille screamed, "Why me? Why does this keep happening to me?" Camille tried to look back on her life searching, for an explanation as to why she kept getting involved in abusive relationships. This time, it had and she wasn't involved in one.

Finally, Camille saw a newer model black and white colored Chevy slowly turn the corner. Peeping out of the window, she could see the head lights on the car suddenly turn off as it neared her home.

Turning the patrol car lights off, officer McIntosh and his partner pulled in front of the cozy English styled brick home. The lawn was sculptured and the walkway was bordered on either side with flowers that glowed a brilliant orange, even in the moonlight. The bent over figure leaning against the rails in a somewhat haggish bathrobe, lifted her head slowly but with and told the officers she was indeed the victim waiting for their rescue.

Approaching her cautiously, while checking for signs of any activity inside her home, the officers verified the address and asked how they could be of assistance.

"What do you mean, how can you be of assistance? Camille shrieked at the officers. "Look at me. Look at me. Look at my face. I can't believe you. You pull up here after almost an hour and now you want to know how you can be of assistance. You can start by arresting the bastard that did this to me," she said. Camille then removed the towel from her head and exposed the open wound on her forehead.

Realizing that a few curtains in the window of a home across the street had moved to the side, Camille became more aware that she was outside where everyone would probably know all of her business by morning. Holding onto the porch rails and trying to weakly pull herself up, she motioned for the officers to come inside.

"We have to check to see if the suspect is still inside," officer McIntosh warned her.

"No he's gone. I know he is," Camille told them.

Peering through the brilliant colors of the stained glass window with the light from inside shining through, officer McIntosh responded. "I'm sure he is ma'am but we need to verify for our own safety as well."

"Go ahead, Camille said, in a haughty tone. If he were still here, he'd be dead by now or maybe I would."

Holding Camille's elbow as he helped her into her home, officer McIntosh noticed the sweet scent that seemed to float off Camille as a slight breeze came through. Though she looked garish, there was something still inviting and attractive about her.

"Do you mind waiting here while we take a look around? He asked her

"No, whatever, just do what you have to do!" Camille said angrily.

Pausing for a few seconds, McIntosh looked the victim in her eyes, at least the beautiful brown almond one that wasn't swollen completely shut, and thought for a moment that he remembered her from somewhere. His eyes wandered to her hips that looked as if they were once luscious and gentle colored.

Feeling self conscious about her looks, Camille looked away when she realized the officer was looking directly at her.

McIntosh quickly adjusted back to his police business attitude and walked through the living room towards the back of the house.

With his hand tightly gripping the handle of his holstered gun, officer McIntosh stepped around the woman and cautiously eased into the home. As he slowly crept into the house, the first thing he noticed was a wall near the entrance of what could have been a den or sun room. The cream colored wall was filled with plaques and certificates neatly arranged in gold colored frames, which bore the name of the victim. Like the opening of an Egyptian tomb, the awards clearly described the victim's path of life just as ancient hieroglyphics detailed the lives of the Pharaohs. Surprisingly, this was the same victim who the officers had stereotypically labeled as ignorant.

A Masters of Arts degree from the University of California Los Angeles in the field of psychology topped the organized honors. Just below that were a Bachelor of Arts degree, a Dean's list certificate and several community service awards stemming from her involvement with a sorority.

Confusion clouded the officer's mind as he tried to understand why someone who was smart and attractive would allow a man to physically abuse her. Until now, he had always thought battered women were mostly poor and uneducated women. Camille certainly didn't fit the stereotype.

As the officer crept further into the house, he observed an old record collection of jazz and underneath that was a modern assortment of jazz, pop and easy listening CDs. Several tables and counters shelved statues of animals and Greek sorority paraphernalia. A ghostly but beautiful picture of Billie Holiday and other female jazz legends like Ella Fitzgerald hung on every wall. There was no sign of her boyfriend in the house, just evidence of class, style and intelligence.

Officer McIntosh suddenly realized why Camille looked familiar and why the name of her street stuck in his mind. He hadn't seen her at the police station. Camille and McIntosh had met years ago, one night while McIntosh was on duty. They exchanged phone numbers and occasionally spoke on the phone. They never made a love connection or went out on a date. Like so many other women he had met, Camille eventually faded to the back of his phone book and then out of his memory. From what he could remember, she had problems with men back then. McIntosh wondered if she remembered him. He contemplated whether he should remind her of their brief friendship, deciding it was not the proper time to reminisce with the victim. Her appearance and what had happened already embarrassed her. Reminding her might cause her to clam up.

Returning to the front steps where the woman and his partner were, officer McIntosh asked, "Why don't we go inside and we will take a report ma'am, okay?"

Turning around, she feebly walked toward the officer. The room began to spin and the floor rolled violently with every step she took. Her head injury was clearly affecting her equilibrium as she suddenly collapsed in front of the officers, face forward on the floor.

"Oops! I think we need an ambulance," McIntosh's partner comically told him.

"Damn! Somebody messed her up good!" his partner added.

"I wonder why she would let someone do that to her? She's not ugly, poor or dumb," McIntosh said, moving to the phone to call for an ambulance.

"I'd do her!" his partner said with no concern.

When Camille regained consciousness, she found herself dressed in a white linen hospital gown. A long plastic tube was pumping a clear liquid substance into the vein in her right arm. At first she thought she was dreaming until her blurred vision focused on a doctor standing at her bedside. Standing directly behind the doctor, were officer McIntosh and his partner. Camille could faintly overhear the two officers whispering and laughing about something.

In a dark and dismal job that dealt with gunshot victims, stabbings and brutal arrests, the battery of a woman seemed humorous to the officers.

"Damn, that was funny. She looked like she had been punched by Mike Tyson and was trying to take a standing eight count," one said.

"Yep! She went plunk! The next thing that I know, she was out like a light."

A nurse interrupted their conversation by saying, "That's too bad. I hope you guys catch the jerk that did this to her and put him in jail!"

"Well it probably wouldn't make a difference anyway. She'll drop the charges and not show up at court. I'll bet'cha." Officer McIntosh added.

Not this time, Camille told herself as she directed her attention back to the doctor.

"You're a very lucky lady," the doctor said. "It's a good thing these fine officers were with you when you passed out. You could have bled to death if they weren't. You've lost a lot of blood. I'm going to have to take a few x-rays before I stitch your head up."

"I know the procedure," Camille mumbled. "I see this type of thing almost everyday."

Camille glanced around the emergency room a second time. On a small metal table with wheels was a plastic bag containing her bloody clothes. When her eyes came back around, she now saw officer McIntosh standing where the good doctor was. The officer was holding a metal clipboard in his left hand and an ink pen in the right. She was glad they had taken her to a hospital where she was less likely to see anyone she knew.

"Where have I seen him before?" she questioned herself, glancing at McIntosh.

Officer Timothy McIntosh reminded Camille of someone. His face looked familiar but all cops looked alike to her. They were all egotistical, angry chauvinists. She knew one once. It was years ago, when she was in college. Camille couldn't remember his name or what he looked like. All she could remember was that he had a bad attitude and felt very negative toward women, especially battered women. Eventually, he had to go! Camille didn't have time for negativity in her life. She had to move on.

"I know that you're not feeling well right now ma'am but I need to ask you a few questions for the report," he said.

Camille stared forward. She was still so embarrassed that she tried not to make eye contact with the officer. She knew the routine all too well. This was not the first time a man had put his hands on her in anger.

"How did I let it come down to this?" she asked herself. "What in the hell is going on?"

DADDY'S LITTLE GIRL

She wanted to be gift wrapped and held by him
and he would tell her...
I am here
I go to work
he spoke solidly
his words sinking deep inside her
and his eyes would question

What more do you want?

He thought of her as a difficult woman
ungrateful even
this ordinary girl
new born needy and really just as typical

What more do you want?
He repeated the question
as she put the raw meat in the black iron skillet
and the hot oil applauded the dramatic
moment

Rhonda L. Mitchell

Camille and her mother have always had a strong relationship, even as a child. Growing up, her mother usually took her to places and events that encouraged her to develop culturally and educationally like Marineland, where Camille learned about sea animals. Mommy was also responsible for getting Camille involved in social activities such as the Brownies and the Girl Scouts which gave her the opportunity to mingle with other girls her age. Not only did she get Camille involved, her mom also volunteered her own time and became a troop leader. Back then, Camille didn't realize the sacrifices her mother made for her.

Mommy took time out from her work schedule to organize and chaperone Camille's Brownie troop on field trips to museums and amusement parks. Their relationship could have been easily classified as special but overall, Camille was a daddy's girl!

At an early age, Daddy's little girl always loved to stay close to her father's side, mainly because she loved the way he spoiled her with attention, gifts and plenty of hugs and kisses. Camille's Daddy took her almost everywhere he went. Most of the time, she would accompany him to an inexpensive department store and watch him comically fumble through the shirt rack in an attempt to select a loud flowered polyester shirt with a wide collar.

Taking the shirt off the rack and then holding it up against his chest, her father would grin and ask, "How's this look on me baby girl? It looks good don't it?"

"Why's it so bright Daddy? How come the collar is so big?"

"That's the style baby. Everybody is wearing um like this."

"Okay Daddy. That looks pretty," Camille would agree.

It gave the little girl a lot of pleasure to be able to take an active part in her father's decisions and activities. Many times, after he'd take care of his business, he would then take her to the toy store where he'd allow Camille to have her choice of whatever toy she wanted.

"Oh Daddy, I want this one!" she would yell with excitement.

"Okay, anything for my baby."

Sometimes her Daddy would let her stay up past her bedtime so Camille could go with him to his bowling tournaments. It always baffled Camille to see her Daddy's personality change so dramatically when he was around his teammates.

"Yeah!" he'd shout at the top of his lungs while squatting and clutching his fist. "Come on baby, get in there, get in there!"

She couldn't understand how rolling a big ball into some wooden pins could cause her normally nice Daddy to jump up and down, scream, say bad words and drink a lot of alcohol. Even though she couldn't understand it, Camille still enjoyed the exciting atmosphere as she clapped and shouted when he did.

Sometimes it was extremely difficult for Camille to believe she was once a Daddy's girl. Although she once was, but that abruptly came to an end at the age of eight. Hurt and bitterness still lingered in her mind as she reflected on that day.

"Look Mommy. Daddy is home!" Camille gleefully shouted as they parked in the driveway after a trip to McDonald's.

With a bag of half-devoured food, Camille quickly jumped out of the car, slammed the door and ran as fast as she could toward the house. Nothing pleased her more than to share food with her Daddy. Opening the unlocked screen door and then creeping slowly into the house, she approached her father who was in the den. Still undetected, she noticed he was comfortably talking on the telephone.

"Daddy must be talking to grandma," she thought to herself. Camille ran to the master bedroom and picked up the telephone receiver. Her sole intent was to join in on the conversation with grandma. Picking up the phone, she quietly waited for the perfect opportunity to yell hello to grandma.

"I love you baby," her father spoke into the phone.

"I love you too, Robert," a soft unknown female voice replied. "When will I see you again baby?" the mysterious voice questioned.

"Oh baby, I've got to go!" her father abruptly said.

Tears began to form in Camille eyes while she breathlessly listened to her father exchange terms of endearment to a strange woman. "Why was Daddy talking this way to a stranger? He never spoke like that to my Mommy. Who was that person? It couldn't be Mommy because she was still outside unloading the car."

Confused and crying, she ran out of the house and told her mother what she had heard. Daddy's words were as disturbing to her mother as they were to Camille.

"Camille, sit down on the front porch and eat your food. Mommy has to talk to Daddy for a minute," she ordered Camille while storming into the house.

Camille tried to focus on the taste of her cold cheeseburger and french fries. She couldn't because the arguing and yelling vibrating from inside the house kept her mind on her father's obvious betrayal to the family. That was the first time Camille had ever heard her mother use the word divorce. That day, an eight year old's father died in her eyes. He was no longer a wonderful dad. In his eyes, Camille no longer seemed like Daddy's little girl.

For a short time, she still continued to hang around her father after the incident but with great suspicion. Every time she went with him to the bowling alley, Camille curiously wondered if that strange female voice she had heard over the phone belonged to one of the many women who joyously hugged and patted her Daddy on his back when he bowled a strike.

In spite of her suspicions and doubts, she never once asked her father any questions about the call nor did he voluntarily give her any answers. On the other hand, Camille and her mother talked about it all the time.

"Does Daddy still love us?" she'd ask her mother.

"Yes! Daddy still loves us honey," she'd try to assure her.

"So why does he love that other woman?"

"He doesn't really love her. He just said that. Daddy loves us."

No matter how hard her mother tried to convince Camille her father still cared, she was still left in a state of confusion. "Why would my Daddy tell someone he loved them when he didn't?" In her mind, it was impossible to tell someone you loved them and not mean it. It was also impossible for him to love someone else and her too. What was going on?

Once, Camille overheard her mother telling her father she was confused and bothered by what she'd heard. She then asked him to explain the situation to his daughter which he never did. Her father refused to believe what his wife was saying, figuring she was exaggerating about how the little girl felt. In Camille's opinion, he was in total denial of the incident and refused to believe she was having a problem with what had happened.

Early one morning, Camille's mother came into her bedroom and softly sat on the bed. Her normally perky mother looked worried. Her expression caused Camille to also worry without knowing why.

"Camille darling, I have something to tell you."

"What is it Mommy?"

"Your father and I are getting a divorce," she said.

"What's a divorce?"

"It means that your Daddy and I are not going to live together anymore."

"What about me and Ricky? Where are we going to live?" she sadly asked.

"You and your brother will live with me. Your father will visit you guys on the weekends," her mother told her.

Tears of sadness leaked endlessly from Camille's eyes as she painfully thought about living apart from her Daddy. She couldn't help believing it was all her fault.

"If I had a wish, it would have been that I had never listened in on my father's phone conversation. If I hadn't, the family would not be breaking up."

A couple of days later, a jolly old balding man dressed in a suit and carrying a large briefcase, came over to Camille's house. Spying into the living room, she saw her mother attentively sitting like a lady on the couch. Mommy's head was straight forward and her legs crossed while her hands gently rested on one knee. Camille's father comfortably sat on the far end of the couch slouching and leaning forward with his legs spread open. The man carefully placed his briefcase on the glass coffee table and flipped it open. Then he removed a small stack of papers and sat them on the table in front of my parents. The sight of the papers caused her parent's eyes to bulge in fear and nervousness as if they weren't prepared to go the distance.

Picking up one of the papers, her mother asked Camille's father, "So what do you think?"

"You can have the house until the kids get eighteen if that's what you want?" her father said.

"What do you want Robert?" she angrily asked.

"I never said I wanted a divorce. This was your idea not mine!"

Lowering her head, Camille silently left her secret observation point and went outside. She couldn't bare to watch her parents bicker. In those few seconds, she could tell her partners weren't leaving one another, and they didn't.

Although Camille didn't see the word divorce applied in it's legal term, she did see it materialize in a more subtle manner. Since both of her parents were postal employees, it was easy for them to divorce each other psychologically by arranging their work schedule so they only saw one another minimally. Her father worked from 3 until 10 while her mom worked 9 to 5 with overtime. Sometimes Camille couldn't help feeling they would have been better off if they'd gotten a legal divorce and moved on with their lives. Even now, she still had a hard time believing married couples are supposed to be friends.

The family picnics and Sunday family outings ceased along with the family trips. This was also about the time her parent's separate vacations started. It was this time period that seemed to symbolize where Camille's problems with men began.

LITTLE GIRLS JUST WANT TO HAVE FUN

Black-girl done good

Black-girl speak
Your voice a hidden flower
the bloom in your throat a garden

Black-girl a comment please?

I cleared my throat
Could you touch me first?

I spoke wit the tongue my eyes
Could you??? Hold me???

My voice throaty and deep
implying seduction, sweetness
My hour had drawn near
and I became a seam
an invisible hem
a simple piping around a collar or sleeve
My tongue unhinged
and a thousand years go by as a moment

and once again
Black-girl is unable to speak

Rhonda L. Mitchell

Camille was only sweet sixteen when she first felt a man's hand ignites a burning sensation within her. Although it was nearly thirteen years ago, she could still vividly remember the incident as if it were yesterday. The jerk's name was Kelvin from what she could remember. He started off as being a nice, fun loving guy. They met at a New Edition concert. He was a cute guy but at that age, there was no possibility of an instant love connection in Camille's young heart, only infatuation.

Like most of her boyfriends, he was a few years her senior. Back then, Camille felt a boy her age couldn't do anything for her. Older guys were more appealing to Camille because they seemed to have more control of their lives and definitely more material things she could enjoy. Her sole purpose of dating an older guy was to obtain wild, immature fun and excitement. Unlike most of the other boys Camille knew, Kelvin had his own car.

Every day, he would pick her up from school and give her a ride home. To have her friends see her get into a car with an older guy was important because it made them think she was mature enough to fit into his world of freedom and choices, something no other high school students had. Also, riding around town in his new "fresh" looking Honda Accord and being his girlfriend made Camille feel extremely important. Sometimes she would persuade him to let her friend Dana cruise around with them. The thing that interested Camille most about Kelvin was that he was a coffee black colored Jamaican. The difference in culture and dialect kept her attention which at her young age was very hard to do.

Camille's relationship with Kelvin was almost perfect except for one thing; her mother just didn't like him. That really bothered Camille because she wanted her mother's approval. Camille wanted her to accept Kelvin and trust her to be alone in his company.

"I want to know why an eighteen year old boy would want to hang around a sixteen year old girl and her friends?" her mother often asked. "How come he ain't out there trying to go to school or trying to find himself a real job instead of hanging around you all the time?"

"Relax Mom. He's just trying to have a little fun like us. Stop trying to always make something out of nothing," Camille responded with bewilderment.

"Just be careful honey!"

Once the darkness of night fell, Camille's social activities became restricted to the confines of the family living room where her mother could keep close surveillance on her activities from the kitchen.

Camille's evening activities with Kelvin mainly consisted of them singing along to Bob Marley songs.

"Mom!" Camille shouted. "Come listen to Kelvin sing. He sounds just like Bob Marley."

Every time he would do something she thought was exceptional, say anything funny or remotely intelligent, she'd call her mother into the room to partake in the activity. Camille's purpose of doing this was to prove to her mother that Kelvin was a good, trustworthy and a positive person for her. As time went on, Camille's mother grew more impressed with him or at least she led Camille to believe that. Her change of attitude didn't cause her to loosen up her dating restrictions.

Camille had to have her fun! She went through an extreme amount of planning and effort to elude her mother's curfew rules. With the assistance of her friend Dana, they carefully devised a series of plans that would allow Camille to sneak away during the evenings to hang out at the mall or wherever Kelvin wanted.

"Hey Mom, I'm going over to Dana's house to study. I'll be back around nine thirty tonight," she'd say before walking around the corner and meeting Kelvin.

When that alibi wore out, Camille used, "Hey Mom, I've got a meeting with the year book staff at a staff member's house. I'll be back around eight thirty."

Camille thought she was clever and had everything under control, especially her mother. The world was in the palm of her hands. Kelvin was providing Camille with all the fun and excitement she wanted. Nothing could go wrong, at least that's what Camille thought. Not long after one of their evening excursions, Kelvin threw a wrench in her plans by drastically raising his demands and expectations of Camille.

With a heavy Jamaican accent, he would constantly tell Camille how much he liked her. "A gal, I lika ya!" he'd say. His flattering words made her feel good and confident as though she was somebody important. Then, he'd mess it up by asking her to sleep with him.

"When ya gwon gimme some poom?"

Suddenly, Camille's free loving world became complicated with the pressures of sex. Every time she saw him, she would have to verbally address the issue.

"I'm not ready right now! Is that all you want me for?" she would respond.

Still very much a virgin, sex was not the least bit of a concern to her. Camille wasn't really into messing around either. She could barely remember kissing him. All the young teenager wanted to do was have some fun. "Leave me alone!" she thought. The new element of sex was too frightening. Camille started shying away from all possible sexually enticing situations. Camille wanted no part of it. All she wanted to do was have fun!

As time went on, Kelvin became more aggressive, overbearing and when angered, out of control. Usually she would just shrug it off because she figured it was just a cultural "thang". Jamaicans were supposed to be crazy for love. Anger and rage were his way of showing her he cared. Camille thought.

"He wouldn't get upset if he didn't love me."

Also, in a weird way, she thought it was kind of cute to hear him go off on her with his Jamaican accent. At that time, Camille was actually a tease. Making boys jealous was her specialty. Jealousy was a rule of measure that gave her an indication as to how much a guy liked her. Also, to see them jealous made her feel like she was in control. One day, after he picked her up from school, she looked out the window of Kelvin's Honda Accord and observed a gorgeous, well-built man walking down the street in Jordache jeans.

"Damn! Look at the butt on that guy!" she spontaneously said out loud.

Suddenly, Kelvin screamed for her to shut up. "Bombaclad! Who ya talkin bout like dat? You dare talk bout anutha mon in my face!"

Then out of nowhere, he delivered a low level back hand slap across Camille's face. She was in a state of shock as she wondered why he had slapped her. Camille grew up fighting with her older brother and male cousins so she was no punk. Quickly gathering herself, she pointed her finger in his face and shouted, "Jerk, don't you ever put your hands in my face again or I'll kick your ass!"

Kelvin didn't say a word the rest of the way home. Once she was home, Camille quickly jumped out of the car and ran into the house. Her anger soon faded because she didn't see him slapping her as a big deal. In her mind, she had retaliated back by threatening him. Besides, the slap didn't really hurt much so she knew he still cared.

"Hell, my brother used to punch me in the nose harder than that when I was a kid."

Eventually, neither Kelvin's accent nor his car could hold Camille's attention any longer. After they broke up, Kelvin and Camille still continued to be friends and talk to each other over the phone. Several months later, Kelvin persuaded Camille to come over to his house for a visit. When she got there, she was surprised to learn they were all alone. His parents were out of town for the weekend. As the two sat on the living room couch, they reminisced about the days when they were a couple. During the course of the conversation, Camille casually mentioned she was dating someone else. Unexpectedly, Kelvin stood up and shouted, "Did you give him some poom poom?"

"That's none of your business!" Camille responded.

Kelvin screamed at the top of his lungs and then basically told her enough was enough. She was going to have to give him some.

"Fo get dis!" he screamed. "Me vex. Me na wait no longer. You gwon gimme some poom!"

Standing up, Camille said, "I'm leaving cause you're trippin." Using all his strength, Kelvin pushed her back down on the couch. Holding her down by her throat, he lifted up Camille's skirt and pulled her panties to the side.

"Please Kelvin. Don't do this!" she pleaded.

Tears poured from Camille's eyes. Unzipping his pants with his right hand, he removed his erect penis from his pants and then proceeded to lie down on top of her. The closer his penis came to her vagina, the more Camille cried. Ignoring her plea, he used his penis as a geiger, fumbling around her vaginal area in an attempt to find the entrance. Just as he was about to find the opening, she made another desperate plea.

"Please stop Kelvin. You're hurting me. I don't want to do this!" she said in distress. Kelvin looked deeply into Camille's tearful eyes for a second and then raised off of her. Camille immediately got up and ran out of his house crying.

By the time she had arrived home, Kelvin had already called her house three times and left apologetic messages on her answering machine. Camille never returned any of his calls. Surprisingly, Kelvin almost raping her took a back seat in her mind. During the months they dated, Kelvin had become good friends with some of her friends. Camille worried he would go back to them and lie about her having sex with him. Fortunately he didn't.

Camille knew Kelvin probably thought he was justified in trying to take what he thought he deserved. After all, he earned the right to it by waiting around for so long. Even though he apologized, Camille was sure he wasn't sorry for hurting her feelings and scaring her half to death.

For a good reason, she never spoke to Kelvin again nor has she seen him since. Her relationship with him was her first abusive experience but certainly not her last. Camille's next bad relationship came two years later when she was eighteen.

Only ten minutes had elapsed from the time officer McIntosh and his partner, Officer Estrada had stepped out of the roll call room until they received their first call. Ten minutes was just enough time for the officers to check out a shotgun, taser, radios and keys to a patrol car. Both officers lugged big, black nylon bags containing extra reports and a riot helmet. As they proceeded down the hallway, McIntosh tossed his partner a set of car keys. "What do you want to do tonight partner? Do you wanna keep books or drive?" McIntosh asked.

"I'll drive. You can book."

"Are you hungry?"

Pausing and looking bewildered, Estrada stared up into the warm sky as if he was trying to get in touch with his internal organs. "Um. . . I don't know if I'm hungry or not. I guess I could eat something."

Once at the patrol car, McIntosh carefully checked the shotgun for cracks and malfunctions before loading four rounds into the chamber. His partner slowly walked around the patrol car, surveyed the body for dents and then tested the lights and siren on the vehicle. Suddenly, the parking lot of the station was rocked with a crime broadcast blasting loudly over every officer's radio.

"Any Southwest units available to handle a domestic violence call at 3500 Marlton Ave come in," the dispatcher announced.

All the laughter and smiles that were once on the officer's faces disappeared. Each officer in the parking lot curiously looked at one another to see who was going to be brave enough to handle the call. One officer looked at McIntosh and Estrada and said, "It's in your area so handle it!" McIntosh and Estrada knew the officer was right but the thought of starting off their night with a domestic violence call was a bad sign. That meant they might have to arrest someone before they could grab a snack.

Picking up his radio, McIntosh pressed the que button and in disgust stated, "Three Adam Fifteen, we are not signed on yet but show us handling that call."

"3A15 roger!"

McIntosh quickly placed the shotgun inside the car's shotgun rack and then took a seat next to his partner who had already started the car. As they slowly pulled out of the station they passed many officers who were again smiling, officer Estrada turned toward his partner, took a deep breath and rolled his eyes around.

"Damn! I can't believe we've got a call already. We didn't even get a chance to gas up the car or log ourselves on the computer yet."

Vigorously typing their unit designation and serial numbers, McIntosh nonchalantly said, "Aw don't worry about it partner. It's probably going to be a big nothing. The comments of the call said the person who called the police heard their neighbors arguing and possibly fighting."

"You're probably right. Let's knock out the call quick and then go eat."

Passing a corner occupied by a liquor store and derelicts standing in the shadows, Officer Estrada angrily glared at the sinister transient figures. "Damn! Those guys are up to something partner. I wish we could stop em and see what they're up to. I don't understand why we have to bother with domestic violence calls anyway!"

As the patrol car turned the corner on to Marlton Ave, officer McIntosh used his flashlight to look at each house number. Several middle-aged women wearing cotton aerobic attire casually walked their dogs and inquisitively looked at the officers and wondered what they were up to.

"Okay partner, we are at 3492, now 3494. That should be it down there."

The officers turned down their radios and tucked their many keys in their back pockets so they could quietly creep up to their destination. "Bitch, you better listen to me!" The sound of yelling and furniture crashing against the walls could be heard coming from inside of the house. McIntosh peeked through the side window while his partner cautiously stood by the front door.

McIntosh whispered, "There's a male suspect walking around and a female sitting on the couch crying. She looks like she has a black eye."

Estrada nodded in acknowledgment. Then he removed his flashlight from his back pocket and forcefully knocked on the front door with the bottom of the metal light. "Who is it?" an angry male voice shouted from inside the residence.

Estrada calmly answered, "It's the police sir. Can you open the door so we can talk to you please?"

The man slowly and hesitantly opened the front door about three inches wide, just enough to expose his right eye and forehead to the officer. "What do you want? I didn't call the police!"

Estrada used a great deal of energy to maintain his patience, calm voice and pleasant smile. "I know you didn't call us sir. One of your neighbors called us. May we come in please?"

"Hell no!"

Suddenly, the man attempted to slam the door closed. Before he could do so, the officer wedged his boot between the door. Pressing both hands against the door, Estrada exerted all of his strength into pushing the front door open against the suspect's weight. As soon as the door flew open, officer McIntosh left his covering position and followed his partner's advance into the residence.

"What are you doing in my house?" the enraged man shouted. "I live here and pay the rent. This is my house! You can't come in without a warrant! I know my rights"

Estrada's smile and pleasant tone dissipated into an angry grimace as he put his hand on the handle of his gun. "Turn around and put your hands behind your back!"

"For what? This is my house."

"Put your hands behind your back now!" both officers simultaneously shouted.

The man stubbornly complied with the officer's demands. Estrada then carefully approached the man while McIntosh kept an eye on the rest of the house and the female who was still sitting on the couch in tears. After completing his search without finding any weapons, Estrada gave the suspect more orders. "Sit in that chair and don't move!"

"How can you tell me what to do in my own house?"

The officers knew domestic violence calls were the most dangerous and unpredictable calls to handle. No one ever knows exactly how a suspect or a victim will react. The officers had to take control of the situation or else they could wind up being savagely attacked by both the suspect and victim.

Estrada did not utter another word. Instead, he placed his hand on his metal baton and partially slid it out of its circular holder. Without any further questions, the man quietly sat in the chair and shook his head in disbelief. While Estrada stood over him with his hand still on his baton, officer McIntosh attended to the sobbing female victim.

"Can you come with me ma'am?" he asked with authority.

The woman rose from the couch and followed the officer a few feet into the next room. McIntosh carefully positioned the woman with her back turned away from his partner and where he could keep an eye on the suspect and his partner. The officer focused his attention on the woman's swollen left eye. Her smooth milky colored skin highlighted a puffy, dark purple knot underneath her eye.

"What happened to your eye?"

Pausing for a moment, she answered, "I had a car accident today."

"Do you have a traffic accident report?"

"No, not yet," the woman replied.

"Can you show me your vehicle?"

"No. It got towed away."

"Did your husband hit you?"

"No! I told you that I had an accident. That's why we were arguing cause I wrecked the car."

Officer McIntosh's gut feeling and experience told him the woman was lying. He did not need her permission to arrest her husband. He only needed to observe an injury on the woman and then have enough reason to suspect her husband had battered her. Even though he knew in his heart that the woman was a victim of domestic violence, her well thought out explanation sounded too possible for him to arrest the husband. He also knew that for whatever reasons, battered wives often protected their assailants from the police. More importantly, he knew he didn't give a damn anymore.

"Are you sure ma'am that he didn't hit you?"

"Yes, I'm sure!"

"Okay then, have a good day." Officer McIntosh concluded and headed for the door.

Both officers were suddenly stopped in their tracks by the suspect's hostile remarks. "Get the hell out of my house! This is my house and I can do whatever I want. I'm a man! I can handle my own business. If my wife hits me, I can handle it myself!"

Like the sun rising at the break of dawn, smiles gradually resurfaced on the officer's faces. Turning back around, officer McIntosh said, "Excuse me sir, did you say that your wife hit you?"

"Yes. She hit me and I handled it!"

"Where did she hit you sir?"

"On my arm why?"

"Let me see."

Officer McIntosh moved his head closer to the man's arm. Closely surveying the man's arm, he found a small two inch scratch on his left arm. A smile suddenly appeared on the faces of the officers. Officer McIntosh moved over to the woman and slyly positioned himself behind her.

"Ma'am, I need you to put your hands behind your back for me please," he sternly ordered the woman while placing a firm grip around her elbow.

The woman's eyes bulged from fear and panic as she twisted and squirmed out of the officer's grasp. "No! I don't wanna go to jail!" she screamed.

"Don't move ma'am! Don't make this any harder than it has to be!"

Clamping his grip tightly around her wrist, officer McIntosh reached behind his back, removed a pair of handcuffs from his belt and took his suspect into custody. "No!. . . No!" she screamed while releasing all of her weight and dropping to the floor. The sight of the victim being physically detained caused her husband to pounce out of his chair.

"What in the hell are you doing to my wife?" he shouted.

Officer Estrada quickly drew his baton from its ringer and took an aggressive stance by holding the weapon in his hands like Hall of Fame inductee Hank Aaron at bat. The slightest advancement by her husband would cause Estrada to tee-off on his head.

Gritting his teeth, the officer yelled, "You better sit your ass down!"

The victim sat back down and helplessly watched officer McIntosh drag the woman out of the house by her arm like a runaway bull dragging a fallen rider.

"Ouch! You're hurting me!"

Tears began to roll sorrowfully down the cheek of the husband's face. "Why are you arresting my wife?"

"Because you said she hit you and then we observed a laceration on your arm. By law, we have no choice but to arrest her for spousal battery."

"What laceration?" the man asked. "All I have is a tiny scratch. You can barely see it."

"Laceration, scratch, whatever. It's all the same to me. The bottom line is she's going to jail."

"Screw you! You stupid jerk! I'll have her bailed out in an hour."

Both officers loaded the screaming woman in the back seat of their patrol car and then sped away to the police station. The sound of crying and weeping filled the patrol car and their hearts with a sense of satisfaction. If the incident had taken place several years prior when officer McIntosh was a rookie, he might have felt sorry for the woman and let her go. But, due to the current climate created by the media, leaving a domestic violence call without an arrest could mean heavy scrutinizing by the press, an indictment or job termination if officers had to return to the scene for a homicide investigation. In this circumstance, he didn't care who hit who first. As far as he was concerned, they were equally to blame and both were worthy candidates for jail.

Once they were at the station, officer McIntosh escorted the nervous and trembling woman into the booking cage so she could be put into the system as a felon which placed her in the same rank and cell as a murderer and a robber.

"I'm so scared officer," she sobbed. "I've never been to jail before. I don't know what to do."

"It's not difficult ma'am. All you do is sleep, eat three meals a day and remember not to drop the soap," McIntosh said with a laugh.

"That's not funny!"

"It is to me!" he sarcastically answered. "So, tell me the truth. Just between me and you, did your husband hit you?"

"Yes. He hit me."

"Why did you lie to me?"

"I don't know sir. I don't know."

After booking the woman for spousal battery with a $50,000 bail, officer McIntosh phoned her husband and advised him she had been booked. Thirty minutes later, the victim arrived at the front desk of the police station with a bail bond for the amount and demanding her release. Both officers surprised the victim who was now a suspect by entering the station lobby through the side door. Without warning, both officers firmly grabbed the victim by the wrist and then handcuffed him against his will.

Shocked, the man asked, "What in the hell is going on?
Why are you handcuffing me?"

"Your wife admitted to us that you hit her. You're being arrested for spousal battery on your wife."

"I didn't hit her. She's just saying that to get out of jail. She hit me."

"She's not getting out of jail tonight sir. You're both going to jail. Now you guys can write each other love letters from prison and start the romance over from scratch. Oops! I made a funny," McIntosh joked.

"Forget that! I'm not staying in jail. I have a bail bond in my pocket. I'm bailing myself out tonight."

"What about your wife?"

"What about her?"

If the officers handled one more domestic violence call in the next one hundred years, it would be too soon. Early in their careers, they actually thought they were making a difference and being productive by trying to give battered women advise. Now, they viewed writing traffic citations as being more important and productive than domestic violence arrests. Most traffic violators at least complete traffic school unlike convicted wife beaters who often fail to complete counseling programs as ordered by a judge.

Like most police officers, McIntosh and Estrada could not understand how an abusive relationship evolves. Do women see signs of abuse early on and then choose to ignore them? Or, does it happen overnight? What kind of men beat women, they wondered?

IN THE NAME OF LOVE

She spoke of being desired
a sparkle in the eye of each and every passing
man
she loved for the feel of a stranger's eyes
groping her ass
or keeping staccato beats with her breasts as
she walked

When those men looked, she stared back
bold and straight as midnight
lips parted into a slight smile

This man was different
he didn't stop at just a stare
he danced her dreams before her
and she followed him... willingly

Rhonda L. Mitchell

At eighteen, Camille felt she was coming into her own as a young woman. She had just graduated from high school with honors and would attend college in the fall. Camille wanted nothing more than to be an adult. Because of her studious nature and the privileges she was allowed at home, Camille was already feeling grown. Still, something was missing.

"Where are my adult friends?"

All of Camille's friends were young and confused like her. They were also under the illusion they were adults. Every time she watched them awkwardly assume the grown-up role, it reminded her she was also in their same shoes. Camille wanted to be grown up and to do grown up things.

To pass the summer days away, Camille got a part-time job working at Sears and Roebuck department store as a sales clerk. The money she made was going toward her college education. Independence was a strong virtue of Camille's. Success was her motivation.

Camille met James at a party two months before her high school graduation. Like the others, he was also several years older. It didn't matter to Camille because she was eighteen and a woman capable of dealing with any man of any age. James was a young entrepreneur who owned his own pager company that he operated out of his studio apartment. After they exchanged phone numbers, Camille told him she couldn't go out with him until after graduation. At least twice a day for the next two months, James called her. They talked for hours. He was so mature and smart. He knew all the right things to say and all the right buttons to push. Soon, she became addicted to the sound of his voice. Camille was already hooked on him before their first date.

When the time finally arrived, she was so excited she could hardly comb her hair. James didn't disappoint her. First, he bought her a beautiful bouquet of roses. Next, he took her to a seafood restaurant where Camille experienced her first candle light dinner. Then, James capped the night off by singing Camille a love song he wrote specially for her. Camille was totally swept off her feet. James was like a dream come true. He was Camille's prince charming. From that day forward, their romance took off in a whirlwind. If she only knew then what she knows now. Looking back, Camille could see the whole control thing starting from the onset.

Over and over, day after day, she would hear James tell her he loved her and wanted to spend every waking day in her arms. That wasn't possible because Camille's time was split between her part-time job and

James. In his opinion, it was Camille's job that was responsible for them not becoming closer.

Early one morning, Camille walked out of her house on the way to work. Standing in front of the car door was James.

"James, what are you doing here?" she asked.

"I had to see you baby," he replied.

"You know I have to go to work."

"I know baby but I need to talk to you," he pleaded.

"I'm sorry James. I don't have time. I'll be late."

"Let me go to work with you. I have a surprise for you Camille."

Whatever James wanted from Camille, he usually got. Through intense persuasion, somehow James persuaded Camille to let him go to work with her. Once they pulled into the parking lot, James looked into Camille's face and firmly said, "I want you to quit!"

"What?" she asked in amazement. "I can't quit my job. I need the money for school."

"You don't need this job. You've got your whole life to work. You're only working part-time for minimum wage. You can't be making that much. If you quit, I'll give you whatever you need."

"It's not just the money James. I like working. If I don't work, what am I going to do?" Camille asked James.

"I want you to spend the whole summer with me. Whatever you need, I'll get it for you," he concluded.

Camille couldn't understand why she succumbed to his request but like a fool, she did. As ordered, she marched into the manager's office and quit her job on the spot. Camille didn't know it then but when she gave up her job for James, she also gave up a large part of herself. Her job was a symbol of her independence. James and Camille celebrated her liberation by going shopping. As promised, in the days to follow, he took good care of Camille. He gave her all the luxuries any young woman could ask for. Besides showering her with gifts, he gave Camille a key to his apartment. Having a key to a single man's home was like neutering an alley cat. They rarely stray from home.

Being around James made Camille feel mature. The added attention and freedom she thought she had, with the plus of him allowing her to blend into his adult world, gave her a false sense of confidence. Camille could only think of a couple of occasions where she would be with James and a friend trying to participate in a conversation and then realizing, "I'm still just a kid! What in the hell are they talking about?" There were definitely times when no matter how hard she tried, she just couldn't relate.

Seldom did Camille ask James for anything. The things she had were because James insisted she have them. Living without him became unthinkable. Without a job or school, Camille had nothing except James. He consumed her whole life. His friends became her's but not vice versa. He felt Camille's girlfriends were immature and a bad influence on her. James and Camille were literally together from early morning until the wee hours of the night.

The first four months were like a fairy tale. Camille had everything a woman could ask for. She had a man who loved her, gave her anything she wanted and never wanted her to leave his side. The feeling of being wanted was the most important part of her relationship with James. Camille's situation with James was new and an exciting first. The more time she spent with him, the less time she spent at home with her family.

No other man, including Camille's father, had ever made her feel the way James did. As in most families, Camille's brother didn't want her tagging around him. The same went for the other boys who lived on the block. Camille's father only let her cook for him and that was about it. Rarely did they ever have any serious father and daughter bonding. Not since. .

.

While Camille's brother gradually became her father's pride and joy, Camille became her mother's. Often, they would go out shopping until the stores closed on them. She enjoyed buying her only daughter clothes and jewelry. Since James' arrival, it had been awhile since Camille and her mother spent any quality time together doing mother and daughter things. Camille figured her mother viewed their outings as special because she and Camille's father were total opposites.

Camille's father was quiet, passive and an introverted couch potato whose idea of excitement was bowling on Wednesday nights. Except for bowling tournaments, he rarely went anywhere, especially with her mother. Without a doubt, he was a nice guy and a good provider but Camille wouldn't have him and neither should her mother. Not because he was a bad person but because she thought her mother deserved someone who was complimentary to her personality. Judging by his actions, Camille's father felt his role, as a parent was solely restricted to depositing a paycheck in the bank every two weeks and nothing more.

Camille couldn't really fault him for his lack of family participation because he was making a conscious effort to give his children a better life than what he had while growing up in rural Virginia.

Her mother was the one who provided Camille and her brother with all the love and nurturing they needed as children. Her mother was so caring, understanding and such a good listener that Camille felt like she could talk to her about almost anything. Even if she was in the wrong, Camille could always count on her mother to be calm and supportive, never "I told you so!" Unlike her father, her mother was a strong willed urban woman from the city of Detroit. She was a bubbly, vivacious extrovert who loved to be out in public. Sometimes it puzzled Camille as to what her parents saw in each other.

Camille's mother and brother were close but not as close as she was to Camille. Once in a while, she'd fuss and complain that her brother was irresponsible like his Daddy. Sometimes Camille and her brother Ricky would discuss their parent's situation. Ricky would always side with his father, even at times when Camille thought her father was obviously in the wrong.

"Why is mama always trippin on dad?" Ricky once asked.

In Camille's opinion, it was just the opposite. Her father was the one who was responsible for the family's down slide. At the time, Camille was determined not to let her relationship with James diminish to the level her parent's relationship had dropped to.

It was a Saturday morning after payday when Camille's mother burst into her room at around nine. Camille was already awake and dressed because as usual, she had promised James she would spend the afternoon with him. Grabbing Camille by the arm, she pulled her away from the dresser mirror where she was making herself pretty for James.

"Come on Camille, we're going shopping," she said.

"I'm sorry Mom. I promised James I would spend the day with him," Camille answered.

"You can see that no-good nigga anytime. He ain't got no real job. Your family is more important than a man," she shouted.

"Okay ma. Let me call him and tell him I'm going with you."

As she pulled Camille out of the door she replied, "You don't need to tell that nigga anything. He ain't your husband. He don't need to know where you are every single minute of the day. Don't be no fool! Let's go!"

Hastily, Camille went with her mother to Nordstroms department store and shopped her butt off. While they were there, her mother bought her a gold heart shaped necklace. Although Camille enjoyed her mother's company, James stayed on her mind the whole entire time. When the time came, Camille couldn't wait to drop her mother off and head straight over to James' apartment.

Once she was at his apartment, Camille eagerly used her key to open the front door. As she walked in, Camille saw James lying on the bed face up, staring at the ceiling. In those short hours, Camille missed him so much that the mere sight of him excited her. James looked so inviting lying there that Camille decided to climb in the bed with him. As she did, Camille anticipated the warm feeling she was about to get when he would wrap his massive arms around her and gives her a kiss. Before she gently rested her head on his chest, she affectionately gave him a soft peck on his lips.

"Hi baby," she softly said. "I missed you."

The response Camille got from him was not what she had expected. Pushing her off his chest and then rolling on top of her, James straddled all of his

180 pounds across Camille's chest rendering her defenseless. Camille's arms were pinned down at her side. She could barely breathe. Staring her in the eye, he asked, "Where have you been?"

At first Camille thought he was joking. In their four months together, he had never once asked her that question. She searched his eyes for an indication as to if he were joking or not. Her results came back inconclusive. The look on his face was neither of anger nor of humor. Clutching her necklace in his hand, James hit Camille with another question.

"Who gave you this?" he shouted in her face.

Before she could answer, he raised up his hand and used all of his strength to slap Camille across her face. Camille's face burned and her ears rang as she tried to comprehend his next series of questions.

"Where did you get this from? Who gave it to you Camille?" he repeated.

Camille was in such shock that she wasn't able to cry, scream, or answer his questions. **SMACK!** Again his hand collided with the side of her face. Only this time, he hit her with a backhand slap.

"You're going to tell me where you got this from. I'm not gonna stop hitting you until you do." **SMACK!**

Finally, after three more slaps, Camille had either built up enough courage to speak or she had become immune to the pain.

"Who gave it to you?" he asked again.

"None of your damn business!" she shouted back.

SMACK! Camille didn't think it was possible for him to slap her any harder than he already had but the next slap sent a tremendous wave of pain throughout her body.

"My mother bought it for me!" she screamed.

James' hand abruptly became suspended in mid air.

"Don't lie to me Camille!" he responded.

"I'm not lying to you! That's who I was with today. We went shopping and she bought me the necklace! I wanted to call you and tell you but she wouldn't let me," She screamed while in tears. "Call her and ask her if you don't believe me!" she added.

Quickly jumping out of the bed and onto his feet, James stormed into the bathroom and slammed the door behind him. Seconds later, Camille could hear the water running in the shower.

"What in the hell just happened?" she asked herself.

While James was in the shower, Camille started tormenting herself with questions. "How could he love me and then just slap me up like that for no reason? Is it possible to love someone and then beat them?" Only if the love isn't deep enough, she concluded.

The question of what type of man beat on a woman never entered Camille's mind. James was her knight in shining armor. He could do no wrong. Camille on the other hand could. Right then, it became obvious to her that she had failed to make James love her more than he did. If she had done something special then he wouldn't have been able to hit her the way he did. Also, Camille couldn't help thinking she had brought the attack on herself.

"I should have called him and told him I was with my mother. Then, I should have told him that she bought the necklace as soon as I walked in the door," she thought.

James once told her he would kick her butt if she ever hurt him in anyway or if he found out she was unfaithful to him. Camille thought that he was just blowing smoke. There was no way he could hit her because he loved her too much.

"He wouldn't dare hit me," she often thought.

Camille's deep train of thought was interrupted by the ceasing sound of running water. A few seconds afterwards, James calmly walked out of the bathroom in his underwear and holding a wet towel.

"Here!" he said to her as he tossed Camille a wet towel. "Wipe your mouth. You've got a little blood on the corner of your mouth."

Despite thinking she had caused James to get angry,
Camille still didn't like the end result. If he didn't love her then she was through with him. Throwing the towel back at him, she said, "I don't want to wipe my mouth. I'm leaving!" James walked over to Camille, grabbed the back of her head and then roughly wiped her face with the towel. Camille's skin and lips grossly contorted from the pressure James applied on the towel.

"Let me go!" she yelled. "I'm leaving!"

"Shut up! You're not going anywhere. Get up and go in the bathroom so you can wash your face. After I get dressed, I'm going to take you shopping. It'll make you feel better," he said.

"I don't want to go shopping with you!"

"Just do what I said okay!"

As ordered, Camille slowly climbed out of the bed and moped into the bathroom. The cold water from the faucet seemed to soothe the burning sensation present in her face. Looking into the mirror, she saw that her cheeks were fiery red but not too swollen. Thank God there wasn't any swelling around her eyes. She would have had a hard time trying to explain that to her mother. Taking a deep breath, Camille closed her eyes for a second and tried to gather herself.

"Damn! I can't believe what just happened."

When she finally came out of the bathroom, James was completely dressed and impatiently standing by the front door jiggling his keys. At that moment, her mind was crossed between anger, disappointment and hurt. She couldn't believe he actually thought taking her shopping would alleviate the pain she was feeling. Camille's first thought was to grab her purse, walk out the door, jump in her car and go home. But, for some demented reason, Camille felt sorry for James.

"It was my fault. He didn't really want to slap me. Even though he didn't apologize, I know he is feeling badly about what he did. Why should I make him feel worse by denying him the opportunity to make it up?" she rationalized.

So for the rest of the day, Camille pretended to be excited and happy about trying on dresses and shoes for James while he ultimately decided what she liked. That day, Camille came home with three dresses and four pairs of shoes. From that point on, she was always careful about what she said to him. All new items of clothing and jewelry were carefully explained. Every minute of her time was accounted for. Camille still loved him but now the element of fear was tossed in. Two months went by before their next incident of violence took place.

Camille's first semester of college was going to start in two weeks. Her girlfriend Tracey, whom she had known since the third grade, was getting ready to leave the state to attend Spellman College in Atlanta. Tracey was Camille's "ace boon coon" before James came into her life. They did everything together including double date. Once, Camille asked James to set one of his friends up with Tracey so they could double.

"Hell no!" he responded

"Why not?" she asked.

"Because she's not their type. Your friends are too wild and loose."

"How do you know that when you've never met any of them? If all my friends are wild, what does that say about me?" she questioned.

"I can just tell that they are not good influences on you. I don't want you hanging around them," he replied.

Of course Camille complied with James' request. Almost a whole summer went by without Camille seeing Tracey and other friends. Although it bothered her not to see them, Camille figured since James was older and supposedly wiser, he knew more and was only looking out for her best interest. Tracey phoned Camille two days before her departure to Atlanta.

"Hey girl! How you doing? I ain't heard from you all summer," she said.

"That's cause you ain't called. How you doin?" Camille answered.

"I'm fine," she said. "I heard that you all in love with some nigga and can't call nobody."

"Who told you that? Don't nobody know my business!" Camille answered.

"Your ma'am told me. I saw her the other day at the market. She told me you all in love with some sugar daddy."

"Girl, don't listen to my mother. She's trippin. It's not like that at all."

"Well, the reason I called is because me and a few of the girls are going down to Venice beach tomorrow and kick it before I leave for school. We want you to come."

Regardless of what James thought, there was no way Camille could refuse to see her best friend before she left. "Okay. I'll go. In fact, I'll even drive," Camille replied.

"Alright then, I'll see you tomorrow about noon." Tracey concluded.

Before Camille picked up her friends, she called James but he was not home. To protect herself against his anger, Camille left a detailed message on his answering machine. The message carefully explained where she was going, whom she was with, why she was going and approximately what time she would be back. Camille then ended the message with, "I love you baby!"

The sunny, ninety degree weather was perfect. Camille and her girlfriends spent the entire day walking on the beach in shorts and tank-tops. The majority of the time was occupied by joking and talking about men, past and present.

"So who's this guy you've been spending so much time with Camille?" she was asked.

Camille proudly boasted to them about her new love. She wanted them to envy her. "His name is James," she answered. "He's real cool."

"So when do I get to meet this guy?" Tracey asked.

"I don't know. Maybe sometime next week."

"Next week?" Tracey questioned. "I don't have until next week. I'm leaving for school tomorrow. How about after we leave here?"

"Don't know. We'll see," Camille answered.

Eventually, the sun set and a dark cloud moved across the beach, giving them the indication it was time to leave. On the way home, Tracey continued to bug Camille about meeting James. Maybe it wasn't such a bad idea for them to meet James tonight. Camille wanted James to be as much a part of her life as she was his. Sometimes Camille thought she was too much a part of his life. She spent more time visiting his relatives than she did her own.

"Now would be the perfect opportunity for James to not only meet Tracey but some of my other friends. Once he meets them he will like them and realize they are good people," she thought.

"Come on Camille, we want to meet him!" Tracey insisted.

"Okay, I'll tell you what. I'll take you guys to meet my man but if one of you try and steal him from me you'll be sorry," Camille jokingly said.

"If he's as fine as you say he is I ain't gonna make no promises," one shot back.

By the time the girls arrived at James' apartment, the weather had changed considerably. By now, Camille's legs and arms were freezing which caused her nipples erect. Scrambling through her purse, Camille took her keys and proudly unlocked James' front door.

"Aw shoot! She's got her own key," someone screamed. They looked at each other and in unison, screamed, "D.A.A.AMN!"

Camille felt big because she had it like that.

Upon opening the door, Camille saw James standing in the middle of the apartment, facing the door with both of his hands secured in his pants pockets.

"Hi baby!" Camille squealed with excitement.

James didn't greet Camille with the same intensity of affection. Instead, he firmly grabbed her by the arm and pulled her into the restroom. "Come here Camille. I want to talk to you!" he demanded as he closed the bathroom door behind them.

James' studio apartment wasn't exactly located in Trump Towers. It was small and wide open. The bathroom was the only secluded and private place in the apartment. Even there, a person's privacy was limited. A fart while making a bowel movement could easily be heard in the hallway by a passing tenant.

"What in the hell are you doing?" Camille asked in anger.

"Where did you guys go?" he asked.

"I left a message on your answering machine. Didn't you get it?"

"Yeah I got it. Were you out looking for guys?" he asked.

The atmosphere in the room was tense. It was like DeJa vu'. There wasn't a doubt in Camille's mind that she was about to get hit. Suddenly, James grabbed her tank-top and tightly twisted it around her neck.

"Why are you wearing this? You look like a tramp!" He shouted at the top of his lungs.

SMACK! The force of his hand caused Camille's head to catapult to the left. The acoustics in the bathroom seemed to magnify the slapping sound. It was an unmistakable sound that echoed through the entire apartment. Pain was not the primary issue. Camille was so embarrassed by the noise that she silently prayed to God her friends somehow weren't listening to what was going on. Only a miracle could have prevented that from happening.

"How come you're not wearing a bra? **SMACK!**

The impact of the backhand slap forced her head back to the right. Using both hands to cover her mouth, Camille tried to hold in the tears and screams of pain. She held in all of the comments and remarks she had for James because she didn't want the escapade to linger on any longer than it had to.

"Just hurry up and get it over! Damn! I messed up again! What is wrong with me? How come I can never make a man happy?"

It was becoming harder and harder to deal with James. Whenever Camille tried to be herself and have fun, she would screw up.

"Why aren't you wearing the clothes I bought you? Huh?" **SMACK!** Two slaps later, James shouted, "When I come back, I don't want to see you wearing that junk and I don't want to see them in my apartment!"

He then stormed out of the bathroom. A few seconds afterwards, she heard the front open and then violently slam close. Taking a seat on the toilet lid, Camille silently sobbed. She was so embarrassed that she wished she could crawl through the faucet and disappear down the drain forever. "How can I face my friends after bragging and then this happening?" Turning on the water, Camille gently splashed cold water on her face until all her tears were gone. After that, she wiped her face, took a deep breath and then opened the bathroom door to face the music.

The room was silent. Every one of her friends was still standing in the same spot as before she went into the bathroom with James. It was as if time had stood still and waited for Camille to finish getting her butt kicked.

"As if nothing bad had happened and we were having loads of fun, she asked, "Well, are you guys ready to go?"

No one said a word. Everyone just turned around and filed out the door. No one spoke of the incident during the ride home. Camille's girlfriends just continued to reminisce about the old days. Camille could tell they were trying to pretend they didn't hear anything. James had just humiliated her eternally in front of her best friends. Still, through it all, it wasn't his fault.

"I never should have pushed his buttons by not wearing a bra and by bringing unwanted guests into his home."

As soon as Camille dropped her last girlfriend off, she headed straight home and phoned James. Tearfully, she begged him for forgiveness. Camille tried to explain that her actions weren't that of betrayal. The only reason she went with her friends was because Tracey was leaving for college.

Camille's explanation didn't go over too well with James. On several previous occasions, James had clearly expressed his opposed views of a need for higher education. In his mind, there was no need for anyone to attend college. If a high school education was enough to boost him to where he was then a high school diploma should be enough for her also. His brothers and sisters were not as fortunate as he was to finish high school. They were forced to drop out at an earlier age because of obligations to their families. It was no wonder why he couldn't comprehend Camille's desire to go on with her education.

For Camille, college was a must. Ever since she was a young teenager, Camille wanted to be a psychologist. She had a desire to understand why people behave the way they do. To achieve her goal, Camille needed to continue her education.

"You don't need college Camille. Don't I take good care of you?" he would say. "You can work for me," he finished.

August 21st was registration day for college. Early that morning, James phoned Camille.

"Hey baby, let's go to an early matinee movie," he said.

"I can't James. You know I have to register for school today," she replied.

"What time do you have to go?" he asked.

"Well, I have to be there at one o'clock this afternoon."

"Good. That leaves us plenty of time. We can go to a movie and then leave there and go to register," he told her.

"You don't have to go with me. We can go to the movies after I'm done." James' mind was set on escorting Camille to school. There was no way she could turn his persistent invitation down. Having James tag along really bothered Camille, especially since she knew he didn't have a positive interest in her quest. Camille honestly believed he came along just to verify her enrollment.

School started the following week. The school she attended was only twenty minutes from her home but a full load of classes limited her time with James. Most of Camille's time was spent going to school during the day and intensely studying at night. Although she missed being around James, talking to him and holding him, it felt good to finally do something on her own and for herself. In the last couple of months, everything she did was in the name of James. She rarely did anything for Camille.

As the school semester progressed, James grew meaner and more possessive. He couldn't understand or believe Camille could spend several hours studying in the school library on weekends. Of course he assumed she was out flirting around the college campus. Looking back on it, subconsciously he was afraid his control was slipping away from him.

During Camille's eager quest to achieve adulthood, James misled her into thinking he was trying to aid in her journey. She misunderstood why he offered her his guidance and advice. In reality, he was trying to mold her into the type of woman he wanted. He didn't want her to naturally develop into her own self. Camille needed school to stay focused on who she was and where she wanted to go.

On more than one occasion, James accompanied Camille to class. It never failed. Every time he got tired and restless, he'd huff, puff, squirm in his seat and embarrass Camille by loudly saying, "Let's get out of here!" He would do this right in the middle of a lecture. Again, he was trying to keep a watchful eye on Camille or he was attempting to deter her from her goal.

On the flip side, Camille began to think that maybe she was neglecting him. Every now and then, despite her hectic schedule, she would go over to his apartment to cook dinner and clean up.

More than once, he said, "Camille baby. Let's have a baby. I want you to be the mother of my child." His reasoning for wanting her to bare his child was first, he loved her. Secondly, he was getting older and he was the only male in his family who didn't have children.

A baby? The last thing Camille wanted was a child. With a child, she would unquestionably have to give up school.

Why would she want a baby? She was still new to the sex game. She wasn't even at the stage where she was enjoying it properly. It wasn't love making yet. It was still only a sexual act she did to please him.

Again, as Camille looked back, she could see that this was another area of control he wanted to take her into. James was trying to contain her in his life forever at some level. Camille's love for him was deep but she never lost sight of the fact that there was a remote possibility that one day (God forbid), they may not be together forever.

"I'm not ready to have a baby honey. I'm afraid," she responded over and over again.

Even though he always used a condom during sex, Camille immediately went on the pill without his knowledge. She didn't trust James because he was set on getting whatever he wanted. As it turned out, Camille wasn't the only one who didn't trust him.

Mothers always seem to know everything. Camille had nothing but positive things to say about James but for some reason, her mother hated his guts. Every time she would ask her why, she'd only say, "I just don't like him. It's something about that nigga I don't like." Camille never knew exactly how much her mother didn't like James until their family reunion in October.

Every other year, Camille's family from the East and the West coast would come together for a weekend of festivities. Camille was especially excited because the reunion was taking place in her city. Camille and her mother, along with one of her aunts, planned the whole event. Every time she would talk to James she'd mention something about the reunion. Camille couldn't wait for James to meet her whole family, especially since she had already met his. If someone in his family had so much as a birthday party for an infant, James would take her along with him. That made Camille feel special and wanted.

The night before the first festivity, Camille asked James to take her shopping so they could buy matching outfits. Camille thought they would look cute dressed alike. As asked, he bought them a different outfit for each day. When she got home, Camille proudly displayed her outfit on her bed. She then excitedly called her mother into the room so she could see them.

"Look at what James bought me!" she said with vigor.

Camille's mother looked down on the bed and then rolled her eyes at Camille. Pressing her lips tightly together, she mumbled, "Um hum. . ."

"James bought himself three outfits like mine. We're going to dress alike at the family reunion," Camille said.

Her mother's eyes almost bulged out of her head. "Oh no you're not!" she yelled. "You ain't bringing him to our family reunion!"

"Why not?" she asked. "He hasn't done anything to you."

"I don't like him! If you want to date him that's your decision but I ain't letting you embarrass me by introducing that nigga to your grandmother! She'd have a heart attack."

"But I've already told him about it and he bought new clothes especially for it Mom," she whined in disappointment. "Why not? He hasn't done anything to you."

"I don't want him there and that's it!" she firmly stated. "If I see him there, I'm going to call the police and have him arrested for trespassing. If you can't come without him then I'll tell your aunts and uncles you love this old man more than you love your own family," she concluded.

Her anger and persistence took Camille by surprise. Rarely did she ever put her foot down so forcefully. Perhaps it was by chance or maybe it was carefully planned out but she had put Camille into a terrible dilemma. There was no way she could miss this reunion and the last thing she wanted to do was to make James upset by telling him he couldn't go. The decision was still weighing heavily on Camille's mind as she dialed James' phone number.

"Hello James?"

"Yeah baby what's up?" he calmly asked.

Pausing for a moment, Camille gave her answer a little more thought. "Promise me you won't get mad okay?" she pleaded.

The mere question seemed to spark a tone of anger in his voice. "What is it Camille? What do you want to tell me?" he asked with hostility.

"Well, I really want you to come with me to the reunion tomorrow but my mother said I couldn't bring you."

Very calmly he asked, "So what are you going to do?"

"Baby, I have to go tomorrow. It's been two years since I've see my aunts and uncles," Camille cautiously answered.

Camille's answer ignited a rage of anger. This was one of the rare times she was glad to be out of his presence. She was sure he would have reached through the phone and slapped her if it were possible. Instead, he battered Camille with harsh words that hurt her far more severely than any of his beatings.

"I can't believe you!" he screamed into the phone. "I take your stupid butt everywhere I go and you can't take me one place with you. Screw you Camille! Forget it! You're selfish. I do everything for you and you don't do nothing for me. I'm tired of trying to make this relationship work. And, I'm sick and tired of your mother trying to come between us. If she wants you all to herself that badly then she can have you! I'm through with you! Don't ever call me again or you'll be sorry! I promise you. You'll be sorry," he shouted slamming the phone down. **CLICK!**

Just like that, Camille's fairy tale relationship ended. She wanted to call him back and plead her case but she was afraid James would get more upset and ruin any chance of her getting him back. Although she believed she loved him, in some ways she felt relieved it was finally over. Camille had grown to be very afraid of James. A big part of Camille wanted her independence back but a bigger part of Camille found it hard to let go of him. James was literally her world.

In the following weeks, she grew more depressed as the feeling of loneliness sunk in. James had left her devastated. Camille's world as she knew it had ended. She no longer knew how to communicate or relate to anyone other than James, his friends and family. It would have been awkward for her to continue hanging around his circle of friends without him.

"Thank God, I still have my family and school."

In between crying, Camille focused hard on her studies. Unfortunately, the theories of Freud and Gestalt were no match for the hold James had on her. Camille's activities around the house were limited to the hearing distance of her telephone. She didn't want to miss his call. Camille would rush home from school each day to check her answering machine. Nothing! Until one day she walked into her room and saw the red light on her answering machine blinking. Call her crazy, but it was something about the way the light was blinking that told Camille this was the message she'd been waiting for. Her hands trembled and her heart palpitated with anxiety as she pressed the play button on the recorder.

"Hello Camille." A deep voice said. "This is Tony. James' cousin. The reason I'm calling you is to invite you to a party I'm having tomorrow. . ."

This wasn't exactly the call Camille had been waiting for; or maybe it was. All sorts of thoughts swirled in her head as she intently listened to the message. First, Camille wondered if Tony knew she and James were no longer together?

"Hum. . . maybe James told him to invite me because he wants to see me again," she speculated. "James must have master minded a plan for us to coincidentally bump into each other. That way, he wouldn't have to bruise his ego by calling me himself and letting me know he missed me."

"So will I see you there?" he asked.

"Thanks for inviting me," Camille replied. "You'll definitely see me there tomorrow evening. Bye."

Camille wondered how she should approach the evening. "Should I play hard to get? Or, should I just walk up to him and immediately apologize for hurting his feelings."

The bottom line was she wanted him back and was almost ready to do anything to get him back, including beg.

A full hour had passed and Camille was still standing in front of the mirror trying to make herself look beautiful for her encounter with James. Camille's dress was fitting her nicely. Snug, but not too tight. She didn't want to look sleazy but she wanted James to realize what he was missing. Holding in her stomach, Camille straightened up her shoulders so her breasts looked fuller. Then, she slowly turned around in a complete circle counter clockwise and gave herself the once over. She was ready. Camille looked good! Grabbing her little purse, she strutted out of the house and gracefully got in her car.

Camille was so excited she could barely hold onto the steering wheel on her way to the party. Her heart had ached too long without James. She missed her baby. Even in his absence, she still loved him as much as she ever did. To Camille, they never broke up. It was as if he'd been out of town on business or something. She couldn't wait to see him. He had to feel the same.

As Camille pulled up in front of Tony's house, she saw Tony and several of his friends standing outside of the party greeting guests as they walked in. Before she could turn off the engine and step out of the car, James' friend Charles approached her with a big smile. Charles was a nice looking man. He was not as old as James. Once, James made the outrageous accusation she was flirting with Charles.

"Hey, Camille. . . How are you?" he cheerfully asked.

"Oh I'm doing fine. How about you?"

"Great! Just great! It's good seeing you again," he said while looking through the window and down at the split in her dress. "You're looking real good!"

Out of the corner of her eye, Camille could see another person slowly walking toward the car. Naturally, Camille assumed it was another one of James' friends coming to greet her. Unconcerned, she didn't turn around. The person approaching didn't walk directly up to the car as she had expected. Instead, he just kind of stood back in the shadows and observed her conversation.

"You know, I've been thinking about you Camille," Charles continued.

Grinning from ear to ear, Camille responded by asking, "Oh really? Is that right?"

Unexpectedly, the person abruptly moved forward and sternly said, "Camille, I need to talk to you."

Immediately, without turning around, she recognized the voice. It was James! Camille's heart filled with excitement as she tried to downplay her emotions by nonchalantly turning around.

"Oh? James it's you," she said, pretending to be surprised.

He looked troubled as if something terribly important was weighing heavily on his mind. Uncharacteristically draped around his shoulders was a small black nylon duffle bag that he sometimes used to carry his work equipment in. Initially, Camille thought it was odd for him to bring his bag with him to a party. Then she figured he might try and make a sale or two while he was there.

"Okay sure we can talk. Let me park my car," she responded.

Faster then she could reach the key in the ignition and turn the car off, James boldly reached through the passenger window, unlocked the rear passenger door and quickly jumped in the back seat.

"What are you doing?" she asked with astonishment.

"I told you I wanted to talk to you. But, I don't want to do it here."

"So where do you want to go?" she asked.

"I don't know!" he yelled in frustration. "Just drive! I'll know the right spot when I see it."

"I don't want to go anywhere. Get out!" she shouted.

As the tension continued to build inside of the car, nervousness, fear and paranoia also began to rattle within Camille. By glancing every so often in the rear view mirror, she could see James fidgeting around in the back seat. After several seconds of fumbling around in his duffle bag, James pulled out a small 38. caliber revolver. Through the mirror, Camille couldn't exactly tell what his facial expression was but the tone of his voice seemed to be quite calm.

Gently pressing the barrel of the gun against the base of her skull, he said, "I have a gun Camille. I don't want to hurt you because I still love you. All I want to do is talk to you but if you try to jump out of the car I'll shoot you."

It seemed impossible for Camille to feel both terrified and excited to be in his presence but she did. To her, his anger, rage and possessiveness was just another natural and uncontrollable urge like hunger and thirst. James had conditioned her to the point where she didn't see those things as a major problem.

Not having any idea as to where she was going, Camille arbitrarily drove southbound on a main street. Although she still continued to glance in the rear view mirror, she was extra careful in avoiding bumps and potholes in the road. The last thing she wanted to do was hit a pot hole and cause James to accidentally shoot her in the back of her head.

About a mile into the drive, Camille stopped for a red light. Occupying a nearby corner was an inexpensive overnight motel. The effort she put into not acknowledging the motel was more than obvious. Sitting emotionless in her seat, she stiffly stared forward out of the front window.

"No, not there! Please don't tell me to go there!" she thought.

"Turn in there!" James yelled.

Pretending not to see the motel, Camille turned her head in the opposite direction and asked, "Turn where?"

"Turn right there!" he shouted as he momentarily moved the gun away from her head and used the barrel to point to the motel. Out of love and fear Camille complied with his demands.

"Now get out of the car and go get us a room!" he told her.

"I don't want to get a room James. I wanna go back to the party," Camille whimpered.

"I told you not to worry. All I want to do is talk to you. That's all," he explained.

"Why do we have to talk inside of a motel room? Why can't we talk somewhere else?"

In the blink of an eye, his calmness turned into anger. "Look! I said go get us a room. If you don't, I'll shoot you right here!. . . Now get out the car and get us a room. And make sure it's for the whole night!" he concluded.

"Damn! Should I run? Or, maybe I should scream for help? If I do, I'm almost certain he will shoot me in the back."

Fear caused the outside of Camille's body to tremble. What she thought was the feeling of love was so overwhelming that she actually wanted to stick around and hear what he had to say. In a weird way, Camille was actually flattered. She had always admired James for being a strong person who had "the juice" and lots of respect from his peers. To be his woman meant she was also important. They were a team. Kind of like Bonny and Clyde, a tough pair.

Camille just looked at this incident as another way to take control.

Exiting her car, she walked up to the outside cashier counter and slipped her money through the slot of the darkly tinted two-way mirror window. By speaking loudly into the round, silver metal speaker, the reservation of the room was completed. Then, the unknown cashier slid a gold colored metal key on a big, bright orange plastic key ring out of the slot. With the key in hand, she briskly walked back to the car where James was waiting.

"Did you get a room?" he asked.

"Yeah, I got one. Now what?" she questioned.

"Let's go and talk."

While they were walking to the room, Camille couldn't help but notice he still had the duffle bag strapped over his shoulder.

"If we are just going to talk then why does he need the duffle bag and the gun? I assured him I wouldn't run so what was up?"

Contradictory to the evening's atmosphere, James used the key to open the motel room door. Then, like the perfect gentleman, he took a step back and allowed her to walk into the room before him. At first glance, the motel room reminded her of her grandmother's house in Detroit. The lighting was dim and the flowered wallpaper, which I'm sure, was once white, was now a dingy cream color. The furniture was made of old wood. Not antique wood but old, faded, cigarette smoke scented wood. As soon as she heard the door close and lock behind her, Camille instantly realized she had made a grave mistake.

"I shouldn't be here! I should have never gone to the party! What in the hell have I gotten myself into?"

Camille's body was so frozen with fear she couldn't turn around and face her fate. Her legs were paralyzed to the extent that the only thing she could do was stand in the middle of the room and stare at a picture of a flower in a vase on the wall in front of her.

"Why are you doing this?" James asked as he slowly walked toward Camille.

"Doing what James? What have I done to you?" she responded with puzzlement.

"Why are you constantly putting me through changes? Do you get a kick out of hurting me?"

The more he spoke, the more irritated he became. His voice continued to sound closer. In seconds, he had moved so close she could feel the hot, wetness of his breath on the back of her neck.

"Why did you come to the party? Huh?" he questioned her.

What was Camille supposed to say? I came for you? Camille knew of no words in her vocabulary could defuse his anger. Her past remarks always seemed to have made matters worse.

Grabbing her by the shoulders with both hands, he roughly spun Camille around so they met face to face. Certainly this reaction will be followed by a slap, she thought. Instead, James moved his head toward Camille and attempted to kiss her.

Shoving him away, Camille said, "No! I don't want to kiss you! I want to leave!"

SMACK! A light stream of blood slowly rolled down the side of her face. "Don't you ever tell me no!" he yelled. "Come here!" he demanded.

Defying his demands, she quickly ran to the opposite side of the room and stood next to the bed so it separated them. Drawing his gun from his duffle bag, James pointed it at Camille. His arms shook from nervous energy.

"This is it! My life is over!" Camille said to herself.

"Get your butt over here!" he said with anger while gritting his teeth.

Camille's feet didn't move. She couldn't tell if her lack of compliance was an intentional act of defiance or a reaction to fear. Regardless, the end result was the same. James snapped. He charged toward her with bad intentions and great determination. Camille's effort to evade him by running toward the door was pointless.

Like a tailback meeting a linebacker up the middle, she was forced backwards and tackled onto the bed. At that moment, panic set in. Screaming at the top of her voice, Camille used every ounce of her energy to squirm and kick her way out of his grasp. James swiftly grabbed a pillow from the head of the bed and shoved it over her face.

"I can't breathe! I can't breathe!" she screamed in panic to no avail.

Surrounded in total darkness, Camille's face was heated by the moisture of her own desperate breathe. She faintly heard James' voice utter something but his words were muffled by the insulation of the pillow. The more she twisted and grasped for air, the more her lungs were deprived of oxygen. The feeling of suffocating was so awful and indescribably horrifying that the only thing that Camille could compare it to was the feeling of almost drowning, which she once experienced when, she was a child.

The assault continued to progress violently as she began to feel the continuous pounding of his fist against the pillow. The pain she felt in her face was so great it was almost hard to believe there was a pillow absorbing some of the punishment. Punches drilled into the pillow and onto her head over and over again until her resistance was overcome by submission.

Except for occasional twitching caused by Camille's hard sobbing, her body lay stiff on top of the bed in darkness. She was totally unaware of what James was about to do. Camille then felt James grab the front of her dress and tug at it with exceptional force. Due to her blindness, she was unable to see the buttons on her dress rip off but the flow of cold air that suddenly hit her body told her they had. Next, he savagely tore Camille's panties from her body. In the same motion, James forced himself inside Camille.

Emotions of anger and hatred were clearly exhibited in James' movements. The more anger he released, the tighter the pillow collapsed around her face. Camille was sure words were spoken but none were heard by her. Her main concern was wondering if her last breath would come from underneath the pillow.

After his last ounce of affliction was discharged from his tired body, James gently released pressure from the pillow. Instantaneously, Camille rose up and gasped for air. She never thought stale, smoky air could smell so good. Looking down at the pillow that was used to smother her, Camille saw that it was soaked with her blood. As she touched her nose and mouth, she painfully discovered her mouth bleeding like crazy. The sight of her blood made her dizzy with shock.

"He loves me, right? Isn't it wrong to hit someone you love? Why did he do this if he loves me?" she thought.

"Stop crying!" James yelled.

"I need to make a phone call," she said to him.

"If you touch that phone, I'll kill you!" he stated.

Camille believed him. James then stood up and moved a chair in front of the door. Taking a seat in the chair, he quietly sat down. James literally stared at Camille as she lay on the bed in tears clutching the pillow until the sun came up. Right before checkout time, James moved the chair aside from the door and told Camille she was free to leave. On her way home she was totally baffled. She kept asking herself, "What in the hell just happened?"

Camille never told anyone what happened. Not even her close confidant, her mother. Despite a couple of phone messages, Camille never saw or spoke to James after that incident. She was too afraid. Camille speculated his next outbreak of rage might kill her. She had too much to live for. Camille couldn't throw it away for a man. She was determined to move on with her life and not consciously let her experience with James interfere with the rest of her life.

An important part of Camille's character and personality was lost during her quest to persevere over the scars of a troubled relationship. She was afraid to be her lively and outgoing self around men. She saw her old personality as a male temper tantrum causing flaw. A more passive and submissive Camille replaced the old problem causing, head strong, crap talker of the past. The last thing Camille wanted to do was cause anyone problems, especially men.

A FRIEND IN NEED

"Who needs them? Certainly not me! I don't need a man nor do I want one!" That was the attitude Camille had adopted at the time she was reacquainted with her friend Tyrell.

"When you don't want them and ain't looking for them, that's when they usually spring up out of nowhere and force themselves on you." Camille had gone over a year without an ignorant male dominating her life. One afternoon, out of the blue, her long time friend Tyrell stopped by her house for a visit.

Camille and Tyrell had known each other since the seventh grade. She had the pleasure of watching him mature mentally and physically from a bony seventh grader to an extremely handsome and muscular collegiate football player. In high school, Camille would enjoy watching him lower his shoulders and knock opposing players on their behinds. Tyrell would always drop by to see her when he was home from college.

Although they had been very fond of one another and dated off and on during the ninth and tenth grade, extenuating circumstances always prohibited them from becoming a serious item. When they were younger, little childish and immature issues such as, "your friends don't like me and my friends don't like your friends", kept them apart. As they got older, Camille and Tyrell were never available for each other at the same time. It seemed like one or the other was always involved in a relationship.

On this day, Tyrell stood at Camille's front door smiling and casually dressed in a tank top, shorts and sandals. As he stood in the doorway, Tyrell confidently displayed his massive arms and legs like Camille had never seen him do before. She couldn't believe his smile, which displayed his perfectly white teeth along with his light brown eyes, still made her blush. Maybe it was because Camille hadn't seen Tyrell in awhile, but he appeared to have gotten a lot bigger and cuter since she'd seen him a couple of months prior.

As soon as he walked through the door, Tyrell grabbed her and greeted Camille with a big squeezing hug and a kiss. Like herself, he was out of school for the winter break.

Camille's face lit up with smiles and giggles as they reminisced about the good old days. For approximately three hours, the two sat on the couch and covered everyone who they went to high school with from A to Z. Several players from their city championship football team were playing at major universities.

"So, are you seeing anyone now?" he asked at the conclusion of the conversation.

"No! How about you?" she returned the question.

"Nope. I'm all alone."

"I can't believe that. I've never seen you without a girlfriend. And now you're a big college football star and in a fraternity, I know you've got plenty of women after you. Come on now!" Camille added.

"Naa. . .! I'm looking for one good woman. That's it," he strongly came back.

"Are you sure you don't have a girlfriend Tyrell? We've been knowing each other for a long time. You can tell me the truth."

Tyrell looked Camille squarely in the eyes and with a sincere look on his face he said, "I'm positive I don't have anyone in my life right now! I've already got your number so how about I give you a call? Maybe we can go out while I'm in town?"

"Hum. . . Should I go out with him?" she thought.

In a fraction of a second, Camille's mind weighed the possibilities. The last thing she wanted to do was start dating again. Camille needed some time off, a vacation from men. On the other hand, maybe Tyrell is what she needed to remind her that men could play a positive role in her life. "Perhaps I should go out with him. After all, how could it hurt? He is only going to be in town for four weeks and then he'll have to go back to school five-hundred miles away."

Besides, it wasn't as if Camille had just met Tyrell on the street or at a social function like all the rest. Camille had known Tyrell since the seventh grade. She considered him to be a good friend and it was sort of flattering to think he still liked her after all these years.

"Oh sure!" Camille excitedly answered. "We can go out."

Tyrell grinned from ear to ear before gathering his composure and gratefully saying, "Thanks, I'll call you tonight around eight o'clock so we can talk about getting together."

As promised, Camille received a phone call from Tyrell that evening. The next day, they casually went to see a movie. The night after that, they casually went to dinner and the following afternoon, lunch. Unexpectedly, Camille spent practically all of winter break in his company.

When the time arrived for Tyrell to leave for school, they affectionately embraced and promised to keep in touch. Just as Camille had speculated, there was no harm in briefly going out with Tyrell. She had fun! Most importantly Camille did it without creating any ties or obligations. Now that Tyrell was gone, her time was again her own.

It all worked out perfectly, right? Not so! During his four-week stay, they constantly bickered about every little thing from what movie to see to where they were going to eat. Tyrell and Camille couldn't agree on anything! At the time of his departure, they both knew the relationship should not progress any further than casual friends, but for some strange reason neither of them had the guts or the smarts to do the right thing and walk away. Against their better judgment, they let the drama continue to manifest, one argument after another.

"Why couldn't I see the signs? Why couldn't I just walk away?"

A strange feeling came over Camille in just two days after Tyrell's departure. For some reason, her attention span shortened and Camille found herself getting easily distracted from her studies. Even stranger was Tyrell kept popping up in her mind without an invitation. What was she feeling? Maybe she just needed some rest? After all, Camille stayed out late almost every night during the last two weeks. Then, an inconceivable realization suddenly hit Camille. Camille missed Tyrell. Not only because she had spent a lot of time with Tyrell but because he was an old friend whom she felt comfortable around, even if they did argue.

"Should I call him and tell him how I feel? Or, should I phone him and say I only called to say hello? I know, I'll write him a letter telling him how I feel. Nope, that'll take too long. I need an immediate fix. Besides, men don't like to receive those kinds of letters," Camille thought.

Whatever decision Camille made, she couldn't do it in haste. The wrong approach could either send Tyrell running scared or give him the false impression she was jocking him. That was probably what he was used to. Camille was sure this was exactly what the other women on his college campus were doing. Camille had to be strong! Her decision for the moment was to do nothing. She had been through worse. After all, Camille was the one who supposedly didn't want a boyfriend.

Around eight o'clock that evening, Camille was sitting at home in her room studying for an exam when her fading concentration was completely broken by a telephone ring.

"Hi Camille. How you doing?" s voice on the other end said.

Camille didn't immediately recognize the male voice. The person sounded like they were calling from an out of state pay phone located at a bar or something. Music, male voices laughing and talking interfered with the clarity of his voice.

"I'm doing fine. Who's this?" she curiously countered.

"Oh! It's like that huh? How soon we forget! Out of sight, out of mind," he yelled.

"Tyrell?"

"I've only been gone three days and already you've forgotten me. Damn! That's a shame!" he said in disgust.

If he only knew. His ears must have been itching when Camille was thinking about him.

"That's not true. I didn't recognize your voice because of all the noise in the background. So, what's up!" she gleefully shouted.

"Nothing much. Same old stuff." Pausing for a moment, he said, "The reason I'm calling you is to tell you that I'm going to be in town this weekend and I was wondering if we could hook up?"

"That sounds nice," Camille responded with a smile.

"Okay then, I'll be in Friday night. I'll call you when I get in."

"Alright! My honey is coming to town," she shouted as she hung up the phone.

Camille felt good and relaxed knowing it wouldn't be long until she would see him. That weekend, Tyrell flew in and then they went out to dinner at a nice, cozy restaurant. This time, the topic of their dinner conversation was more serious than the previous, "Oh, have you seen so and so?" conversations. Anxiety clearly radiated from both of their bodies. Neither of them knew what to say yet they both knew what they wanted to talk about!

"Guess what Camille?" Tyrell asked.

"What?"

Clearing his throat and taking a big swallow, he humbly said, "I missed you."

"Aw. . . That's so sweet."

That was the only thing she could think of saying at the time because his comment totally caught her off guard. Tyrell echoed her sentiments exactly. In addition to Camille missing Tyrell, she was also baffled. Why, after all this time, was she missing Tyrell?

"He's been right here in my face for umpteen years and now, after he moves five-hundred miles and seven cents a minute away, I miss him. How weird," she figured.

"Even though I go to school so far away. I'd still like to see you and talk to you on a regular basis," Tyrell requested.

"That's funny. I was thinking the same thing. It's really weird. This wasn't supposed to happen. When I first saw you again, I had no intentions of getting seriously involved with you but now I find myself missing you," Camille explained.

"I know what you mean. We've been knowing each other for years but I never thought I'd ever have another shot at dating you."

The remark sounded strange coming from Tyrell because she was always friendly toward him. They shared many of the same friends and hung out in the same places. Curious about his reasoning, Camille asked, "Why not?"

"Because you've always seemed so smart and you've always seemed to have your stuff together. Besides, since I've known you, all you've ever dated were older guys.   I kinda looked up to you," he confessed.

"I've always thought you were cute. I use to sit up in the bleachers and cheer for you at every football game."

"So where do we go from here?" Tyrell solemnly asked.

"I don't know. . ."

By the end of the night, Tyrell and Camille had unanimously decided they would take turns visiting one another every other weekend, except during the week of midterms and finals. Their roles in the relationship were not discussed or defined. A full commitment was not mentioned. As far as Camille knew, they were still only good friends.

Camille's mind was now somewhat at ease. If she felt the need to call Tyrell long distance and talk to him which she frequently did, she could call without feeling like a predator. School was now much easier to focus on knowing she would see him in two weeks. Three days before the weekend of their coupling, Tyrell sent Camille a round trip plane ticket to Berkeley, California. She was totally thrilled to no end. Two weeks had almost seemed like two months.

Visiting him was the single most important thing on Camille's mind. "Will I be making a big mistake by visiting him? We really don't get along. If for some reason we do get along this time, without a doubt, it will take our relationship to another level. Do I really want to go there?" she thought.

Tyrell told Camille he thought highly of her because she was a strong, calm and collected person who knew what she wanted.

"Will I be making a mistake by showing him my sensitive side? I don't want him to view me as weak!" she thought.

Friday evening, Camille went into her mother's bedroom and asked her if she could use her big Samsonite suitcase.

"Why do you want my suitcase? Where are you going?" she asked.

The thought of the reason made Camille feel uneasy and strange. Maybe it was too soon. Or, maybe it wasn't soon enough because they may have already let their opportunity pass.

"I'm flying up to Berkeley to visit my friend Tyrell," she told Mom.

"Tyrell?" Camille's mother asked with strong disbelief. "Not that little boy who lives around the corner who use to come over all the time when you were in high school?"

"Yes, that's the one. Only he's not so little anymore. He plays football for U.C. Berkeley."

"Wow! I didn't even know you guys still kept in touch."

"Oh, by the way, I need you to do me another favor and drop me off at the airport tonight," Camille requested.

"Sure. Is there anything else?" her mother sarcastically asked.

Camille's trip was only planned for three days but she still piled her suitcase with three sexy evening dresses, three cute and colorful casual dresses, several pairs of shoes and an assortment of shorts, pants and coats. Camille wanted to be ready for anything. Most of all, she wanted to look cute for Tyrell.

From the time she left her house until the moment the plane landed, Camille's heart remained filled with a combination of joy, anxiety and doubt.

"Too late now", she thought as the plane landed. "I'm here now."

As Camille had imagined, Tyrell was standing in the airport terminal waiting for her with open arms and a big warm smile.

"Hi baby! I'm glad you're here!" he told her.

While enroute to his apartment, Tyrell took a detour route which lead them through the college community surrounding the campus. The majority of the coffee shops and stores were old and funky looking. The atmosphere of the area was totally the opposite of the bourgeois college community Camille was accustomed to. After briefly sightseeing, Camille and Tyrell pulled into the parking lot of an apartment complex located a couple of blocks from the campus.

"This is it!" Tyrell eagerly shouted. "This is home!"

"This looks nice!"

"Thanks. It doesn't have the luxuries of a pool, Jacuzzi or a sauna but it's home."

Tyrell grabbed Camille's suitcase from the trunk and started lugging it to his apartment. "Wow! What all do you have in here? How long do you plan to stay?" he asked.

"Just til Sunday but I had to come prepared for anything and everything."

Camille followed closely behind Tyrell as he opened the front door and walked inside. "Pee-you!" Tyrell's apartment smelled similar to a stuffy locker room. The overall cleanliness of the apartment was fair but the air reeked of musty gym socks. All it really needed was a woman's touch.

"Tyrell I'm thirsty. Can I have a glass of water?"

"Sure, help yourself. My home is your home."
Pointing, he said, "The kitchen is that way."

What Camille found in the kitchen was a lot
worse than the living room. She disgustedly found
dirty dishes piled high in the sink. Stale food odors
generated from the dishes. Numerous bottles of
vitamins and powdered protein drinks cluttered the
kitchen counter. Holding her nose, she quickly moved
past the heap to the refrigerator. Camille quickly
opened the refrigerator door in hopes of retrieving a
glass of water. Inside, she found a half carton of
orange juice, four apples, a jar of mustard and a bottle
of water.

"Shoot! Didn't he know I was coming? He
could have at least went to the store and bought
something for me to snack on! A true backwards
bachelor!"

Before Camille could muster the courage to
drink from a glass, she felt the need to wash the dirty
dishes first. Taking off her rings and watch, she rolled
up her sleeves and began running water in the sink. A
few seconds later, Tyrell heard the water running in
the kitchen and joined her.

"What are you doing?" he asked Camille in a
nasty tone of voice.

"I'm washing your dishes."

"You don't have to do that! I'm going to wash them later!"

"It's not a problem. I don't mind. I'll do it," she offered.

Tyrell frowned his face, took a deep breath and the exhaled. Next, he folded his arms and annoyingly tapped his foot on the floor. For some odd reason, he appeared angry with her.

"Why is he pouting? What did I do to him? I'm only trying to help the trifling idiot. He should be happy I'm cleaning up for his nasty butt!" Camille thought to herself.

"You don't have to do this Camille!"

Turning off the water, Camille replied, "Okay, if you don't want me to do it then I'll stop."

"Forget it now! You've already started so you might as well finish!" he said as he stomped out of the kitchen.

"Dang! What a big baby. Why was he getting so bent out of shape?"

Camille turned the water back on and started working. After busting suds, she wiped the counter down with Pinesol and then neatly organized his vitamins. Now, she felt more at home. Camille then poured some water in a clean glass and moved back into the living room where Tyrell was sitting on the couch watching television. With caution, she took a seat on the couch next to Tyrell. Tyrell seemed to have mellowed out from his sulking mood.

Surprising Camille, he leaned over and gave her a gentle kiss on the cheek.

"Hi sweetheart. I'm glad you're here," he said with a soft smile.

"I'm glad I'm here too," she replied. "I've been thinking about you all week."

"Are you hungry?" he asked. "I don't have anything here to eat. . ."

"No kidding!" she privately answered.

"But, we can go out somewhere and get you something. I'm only eating fruit and protein drinks right now," he added.

Although she was a little hungry, now didn't seem like the time to express it. They just had mixed words. The last thing she wanted to do was be a nuisance.

"Oh no honey. I'm fine. I ate before I came."

Later that night, he again asked her if she wanted to get something to eat and again Camille told him she wasn't hungry.

"I'm not really hungry," she answered.

That was a lie! Camille was hungry and disappointed as hell! This idiot barely had enough water to go around. Camille thought they were going to do fun things like cook their meals together, go miniature golfing or just walk around the campus or something. She was terribly disappointed! Tyrell was also acting weird. Camille was hungry and didn't want to be there anymore! Her big mistake was acting like his crap didn't bother her when she knew it made her feel uncomfortable. Why in the hell was she there anyway?

That had been the story of her life. Camille dealt with crap and pretended like it didn't matter because she thought she was this big, bad, tough woman who didn't trip off of anything. Because of this attitude, Camille wasn't about to show Tyrell a different side of her. She had to continue to be Ms. cool, calm, and collected Camille. After all, she had dated older men. She figured she should know how to handle her emotions and not trip-out over some petty stuff, even if it did bother her.

"Be strong Camille! Don't let anyone know you're hurting! Don't let it bother you!" she continually told herself. Camille used those same words when she was a child trying to deal with the pain and anguish of her cheating father. Her objective then as it was presently, was to internalize everything, lock it away and then try to pretend like it wasn't a big deal. She lied to herself then as well as during her visit with Tyrell.

"I really don't want to eat anything but I'd like to snack on an apple if you don't mind," she responded.

After gnawing the first one down to the core, she told Tyrell, "Boy! That apple was good. Where did you buy those from?"

"The market."

"Do you mind if I have another one?" she asked.

"Go ahead," he said with a bewildered look on his face.

The rest of the night went smoothly without conflict. Camille somehow convinced herself she was elated to be in Tyrell's company. After all, he was intelligent and had a hell of a body. He had the kind of body that made a woman look forward to spending an intimate night with him.

When Camille woke up the next morning, she found herself lying in Tyrell's bed with her head resting comfortably on his massive chest as he slept. Lifting her head, Camille looked around the room and assured herself she was not dreaming. The feeling was so sensational that she laid her head back on his chest and drifted back to sleep. This was so perfect, no conflict, just peace and love. So Camille thought. Her tranquility was suddenly broken by the startling sound of the phone ringing. It wasn't until the fourth ring that Tyrell reached over and picked up the phone.

"Uhm. . . Hello?" he drowsily said. "Oh! Hi. How are you?" he said as he instantly awakened.

For some reason, he appeared to be a little jittery.

"Um hum. . . Um hum. . . Oh, I'm not doing anything. I was just lying here getting ready to study."

"Who in the hell is that and why did he have to lie about studying? How come he couldn't tell them he had company and he'll call them back later? Why is he still carrying a conversation with that person when I'm here?"

"Um hum. . . I can't today cause I got an exam on Monday. . . I really need to study this weekend. I'll call you later, okay?"

After hanging up the phone, Tyrell actually had the nerve to roll over on his side with his back turned toward Camille, curl up and pretend to go back to sleep.

"The nerve of that fool! Who in the hell does he think he is? He's got some explaining to do!"

It was more than obvious to her the person on the other line was a woman. Men aren't that kind and sweet to their buddies unless they are sweet themselves.

"Hum. . . that's a thought. Naw, that was a woman, I know it. Women can tell these things. Oh yes, he's got some explaining to do."

Even though Camille was pissed off, she didn't want to verbally attack him because officially they weren't boyfriend and girlfriend. Although they weren't, she still felt like they were. Camille couldn't talk to another guy or give out her phone number without feeling guilty or feeling as though she was cheating on Tyrell.

Politely nudging his shoulder, she softly said, "Excuse me but I need to talk to you."

Tyrell slowly rolled over, smacked his mouth and rubbed his eyes as if he'd been dead to the world.

"Um. . . What is it baby?" he asked.

"Don't you think that was a little rude?"

Trying to play dumb, he replied, "What? What was rude?"

"I just think you should have told her you have company. That's all."

"Told who? What girl? What are you talking about Camille?" he asked with a puzzled look on his face.

His act was so convincing Camille wouldn't have believed the conversation took place if she hadn't been there and overheard it for herself. His performance pissed Camille off oven more but she was determined not to loose her cool. After all, this was Camille's first visit and she was desperately trying not to cause any conflict.

"Tyrell, I'm talking about the phone call you just had. Why didn't you tell her you had company?" she politely asked.

"Why it gotta be a girl that called? How come it couldn't have been somebody on the team wanting to know if I wanted to workout?" he stated with animosity.

Still calm, she asked, "If it wasn't a female then why didn't you tell them you had company?"

"Because, maybe I don't want people in my business?"

"I could tell it wasn't a man on the phone. I hope you don't talk to your male friends that smoothly."

A small smirk appeared on his face as he said, "You're right. It wasn't a guy. To be honest, it was my mother. I didn't tell her you were here because I don't think she's ready for that."

Camille couldn't believe he went there. His mother? "He must really think I am stupid or something. There is no way in hell I'm going to believe that it was his mother on the phone. But, I don't want any problems so I'm not going to sweat it," she thought.

"Whatever Tyrell! Forget it!" she said in disgust.

Tyrell didn't seem the least bit affected by their discussion. Instead, he lazily rolled back over and went back to sleep. For several minutes, Camille sat up in bed and stared at him in disappointment. Tyrell had fallen from his pedestal. He was no longer the nice, sensitive and caring individual she thought he was. Camille did enjoy Tyrell's company but screw him!

"I don't need this! I'm going home!"

It's true Camille missed him but she and Tyrell hadn't really built a strong need for each other. There was nothing in their relationship worth hanging around. Camille had to get the hell out of his apartment and his life. If she would have remained in his apartment another minute, an argument would have certainly jumped off.

While Tyrell remained asleep, Camille quietly packed her suitcase and then called for a cab. A good bye, you ain't "nothin", why did you do me like that speech would have felt good but it wasn't in accord with her plans. Camille just wanted to exit his life without further conflict or appearing childish and whiny. Or, maybe she did it like that because she didn't want to end it permanently? Camille knew that when he found out she was gone, he would surely know she was angry but not angry enough to end the relationship.

This kind of stunt would give him the opportunity to finally show her how appreciative he was of her. If he didn't care, he wouldn't call. If he cared, he would call. Then when she got home, if she felt like it, she could call him back and pretend like the incident didn't phase her. The bottom line was, Camille had to let Tyrell know she was not the one to be dogged and she could be gone in a flash!

That's what Camille should have done, left Tyrell's life for good. She should have departed in a flash. Camille should have said what she had to say, express her feelings and then stepped! Unfortunately, she wasn't good at any of those things so Camille continued to drive down a dead end street. What a ride it was.

Twenty minutes of self-evaluation had already taken place when Tyrell's apartment suddenly became overwhelmed with the sound of the doorbell ringing. An immense strain was instantly lifted from Camille's shoulders the moment she opened the front door and saw the cab driver.

"It's good to see you!" she told the driver.

"You want me to take that suit case for you ma'am?"

"That'll be great!" Camille happily replied.

From out of nowhere, Tyrell materialized. Dressed in a dingy black robe, he straddled his body across the front door and curiously asked, "Where are you going?"

"I'm going home."

"But I thought you said that you were staying the whole weekend?" he asked.

Briskly walking past him and out of the door, Camille coolly answered, "I changed my mind, bye."

With her head held high and shoulders erect, Camille proudly and confidently strolled out of Tyrell's life, presumably forever. The cab ride to the airport was quick but even more surprising was the flight back home to Los Angeles went by much faster than it had going into Berkeley. Camille gathered it was because the anxiety of seeing "what's his name" was over.

After arriving in LAX, Camille again called for a cab. She could have called her Mom for a ride but Camille didn't want to trouble her mother or anyone else. Besides, if she had had someone pick her up then she'd have to talk about the trip. Camille wasn't ready to discuss it with anyone yet. It felt good to be at home in her domain where she had control and felt safe.

As soon as Camille walked through the door, her phone rang. "Damn, I can't even get home good and the phone starts ringing!" Camille yelled out loud as she rushed to the phone. Tyrell was the last person she had expected to hear from, especially this soon. Somehow, Tyrell timed Camille's arrival perfectly. In her mind, she wasn't completely through with him. She hoped Tyrell felt the same. There was a slight chance he could have surprised Camille and not ever call her again.

"I just called to see if you made it home," he opened.

"I'm here. Thanks for calling and checking," she aloofly replied. "I've got to unpack so I'll talk to you later."

"Wait! There's something else I've gotta tell you. . . I'm sorry for how I acted. I shouldn't have disrespected you by snapping at you. It's just that I'm under a lot of stress right now and I don't know what to do or how to handle it," he explained.

Tyrell then proceeded to tell her that he was having an ongoing dispute with the football coach regarding his position and playing time. He was seriously contemplating leaving U.C. Berkeley, transferring to another school and giving up playing football permanently. The major problem was he couldn't afford to attend college without a scholarship.

Before this telephone conversation, Camille honestly felt there wasn't anything he could do or say that could persuade her to stay in his life but somehow, Tyrell found the right button to push. Good ole Camille, to the rescue again. Always understanding everyone else's crap, especially when they have disrespected and abused her. Tyrell threw out the hook and Camille bit down on it hard.

"He is obviously crying out for my help. I can't turn my back on a friend in need. If I leave him now, it will be like kicking him when he's down and then running like a coward. How narrow minded of me not to have seen his anguish and then sense he had a problem."

"I'm just going through a lot of mess right now Camille," Tyrell explained.

"Don't worry about it honey," she sympathetically responded. "Everything will turn out okay. I'll help you in any way I can."

"I wouldn't blame you if you decided not to see me anymore," he pitifully said.

"I'm not going anywhere baby. I'm here for you Tyrell," Camille assured Tyrell.

"Damn, he got me!" she thought to herself.

Tyrell needed Camille's help and she instantly committed herself to his assistance. Suddenly, Camille had a sense of purpose and a role in the relationship. That was all she needed to keep herself going. Camille believed by helping Tyrell, she was fulfilling his expectations of how a good woman was supposed to behave. Camille was also filling an emptiness in her life. She was going to do whatever she could to help him find happiness. Camille didn't know it would eventually mean she was going to have to sacrifice some of herself.

Monday morning, in between classes, Camille went to her campus admission department and picked up a University of California college application and a financial aid package for Tyrell.

Camille didn't make any plans the following weekend when Tyrell drove down to LA. Instead, she asked him to come over for what he thought would be a quiet evening at home.

"Hi baby!" Camille excitedly said as she greeted Tyrell at the front door with a hug and a kiss. "I've got a big surprise for you honey!"

"Oh really? What is it?" he asked with an animated boyish look on his face.

Leading Tyrell by the hand to the dinning room table, she picked up the U.C. application and handed it to him. Camille was certain her effort would be greatly appreciated.

"This is for you!" she said.

Tyrell's bright expression of glee and joy metamorphosed into a look of puzzlement and disappointment. "What is this?" he asked.

"It's a U.C. application. I figured you could leave U.C Berkeley and transfer to U.C.L.A. It'll be much cheaper and with financial aid you won't be out of a lot of money."

"Who in the hell said I wanted to attend U.C.L.A or get financial aid?" Tyrell angrily shouted.

Camille's breath was totally taken away by his lack of appreciation. Damn! Did I do something wrong? Why is he trippin like this? she thought. "It wouldn't hurt you to fill it out. If you get accepted you don't have to go. Just try it and see. You never know, you might change your mind later," Camille said.

"I ain't filling out nothin!"

"Okay don't. I'll do it for you. . . Sit down!"

Like a naughty child being scolded, Tyrell stubbornly folded his arms and slumped down in his chair. Whipping out a pen, Camille systematically filled out the application by first answering all the questions she already knew regarding Tyrell. This gave him the opportunity to cool down some.

Once he cooled off, she then completed the rest of the application by politely asking him to provide her with the additional information. Getting the information from him was more difficult than getting a serial killer to confess.

After completing the tedious task, Camille and Tyrell quietly sat on the couch and watched television until the wee-hours of the night. Although there wasn't any more mention of the application, she could feel the tension hovering about in the room. In fact, Tyrell's pouting mood put a damper on the whole weekend. He was clearly not his usual cheerful self.

At the conclusion of their weekend, Camille again assured Tyrell everything would turn out fine and first thing Monday morning, she would send off his applications. An expression of gratitude was visibly absent from his face and body language, as he appeared dejected and frustrated for some reason.

The last two episodes with Tyrell were not exactly filled with love and romance. Despite the two negative encounters, Camille still felt compelled to hold up her end of the agreement which was for them to see one another every other weekend. Two weeks later, it was again her turn to travel five hundred miles north to visit a man whom she had questionable feelings for. Tyrell's erratic behavior was a concern. Camille assumed that if she controlled herself then he wouldn't have a reason to get disturbed.

Because she was young, energetic and out-going, she was down for just about anything. The primary focal point of this visit was not to have a good time with Tyrell, it was more of an opportunity to get away for the weekend. It was also a chance for her to do something different, other than going to school and studying.

For five and a half hours, music cassettes blared from Camille's car stereo while she made the tiresome drive up the sloping northern highway. The scenery was monotonous mainly because there wasn't anything to look at on either side of the highway but empty grass fields. The only thing visible when looking forward was an endless grade of highway stretching further than her eyes could see.

Most of her traveling time was geared toward psyching herself up for her encounter with Tyrell by blasting a medley of love songs and slow ballads. Over and over, she played a ballad by vocalist Oleta Adams called "Get Here." Ironically, the melody fit the mood she wished she were in.

Five and a half hours later, Camille arrived at Tyrell's apartment. The long drive had completely exhausted her. She felt totally drained. Within a short time of her arrival, she had no choice but to take a short nap on his living room couch.

Two hours later, she awoke from her restful sleep to the sound of a whispering baritone voice coming from Tyrell's bedroom. A stretch and a yawn were in order as she rose from the couch and sluggishly walked into the next room to investigate. To her dismay, she discovered the voice emanating from the next room belonged to Tyrell as he suspiciously lowered his head and turned his back toward the door. Placing her hands on her hips and spreading her legs shoulder width apart, Camille moved her neck around in a circular motion and then dropped her mouth open in amazement.

Tyrell continued talking on the phone for what seemed like ten minutes. Anger continually built inside her body with every passing moment. The heat from her anger rapidly thawed the awaking stiffness in her body. Spiteful thoughts replaced all the other feelings she felt for him.

"Forget that! I've been entirely too nice and I've done too much for this sorry bastard to let him mess me around! He got off easy the first time but not this time! I'm going to give him a piece of my mind. I don't care if he does get upset! I'm gonna let him know I don't like it and I'm not putting up with this bull!"

Tyrell glanced back at Camille and quickly whispered into the phone, "I've gotta get off the phone and take care of something real quick!.. I'll call you back later!" He then quickly hung up.

"Who were you talking to?" Camille sharply asked Tyrell while advancing in his direction. "What was that all about? Why did you have to whisper and who were you talking to?"

Her bombardment of questions along with her hostile demeanor caught Tyrell off guard. Trying to be nonchalant but stammering, he answered, "Nobody."

"Nobody? How could you be talking to nobody?" she screamed in his face. "Do you think I'm stupid or something? What's her name?" she demanded.

"Karen," he calmly answered. "She's just a friend. That's all."

Tyrell's sudden admission of guilt pissed Camille off even more. Raising her voice two decibels louder and advancing one step closer, she shouted, "Why did you have to lie? How come you couldn't tell me the truth when I asked you the first time?"

"I didn't lie. She is nobody compared to you."

"Forget that! She must be more than just a friend cause you didn't tell her I was here."

In the blink of an eye, Tyrell flat-out sprung up from his chair with the strength and agility of a tiger attacking his prey. His hands viciously gripped Camille's blouse. Fear and uncertainty replaced her fury. Camille looked down and found herself elevated two feet off the floor. Like the force generated from a tornado, her body catapulted backwards. Camille's flight was abruptly stopped by a hard collision with the wall. **BOOM!** Her head and back impacted the wall with so much force the pictures in the apartment shook and the windows violently rattled like thunder.

"Shut the hell up Camille! This is my apartment and my phone. I can talk to whoever the hell I want to!"

Tyrell then accentuated his statement by shoving her against the wall a second time before walking out of the room. With him out of the room, Camille straightened up and tried to make some sense out of what had just happened. Maybe it was because her mind was still in a daze or in shock but the fact she had just been physically abused didn't register.

"Damn! Maybe I said too much? Why did I have to take it that far? I shouldn't have come at him that way. Maybe I was too hostile? I probably should have used a more diplomatic approach. Then, he wouldn't have been so defensive and attacked me the way he did. Perhaps the reason he was so upset was because I was making false accusations? Am I jumping to conclusions? What if she is nothing more than a platonic friend? Damn! Why do I keep messing up?"

Camille was still upset but as far as she was concerned, the fight was over. It was a dead issue. If Tyrell said she was a platonic friend than maybe she was.

"Whatever! I don't care!" she concluded.

Packing her bags for the return trip was considerably easier than her first sudden departure. This time, she never got the chance to unpack. With moisture quickly building in her eyes, Camille swiftly grabbed her belongings and then hurried out the door.

The ride home was extremely tiresome, especially since she was dangerously operating on a two-hour nap. This time, Camille's music repertoire consisted of very few slow songs. Hard, fast bass rhythms vibrated her trunk and windows. Not only did the music soothe her it also kept her awake.

When she arrived at home, Camille walked into her room and discovered her answering machine was blinking like crazy. Without pushing the play button, she that knew at least one of the calls had to be from Tyrell. The first message on her machine was from her girlfriend who wanted to know if she was going to a school dance.

Beep! "Hi Camille. I hope you made it home safely. I'm sorry about what happened. I promise it'll never happen again. I really hope we can work this thing out cause I miss you," Tyrell's message stated.

The next three messages from him were similar in their meaning. It was obvious Tyrell had some serious problems that he needed to deal with. Camille reasoned that he was experiencing a few emotional highs and lows. She figured his frustrations were from his uncertain future.

"Once things are stable, he'll be nice and more appreciative of me."

It didn't occur to Camille that she also had a problem of a different kind. She also needed to clear some things up. Camille's problem was that she desperately wanted to feel needed. Tyrell needed her but the physical and mental price she was paying was extremely high. Subconsciously, she had agreed to pay the price because as her father always said, "Nothing comes for free!"

Camille continued to see Tyrell although his temperament was a constant issue in her mind. Although physical abuse had not yet reoccurred, little indiscreet signs of verbal abuse began to surface. Everything she did was wrong in his eyes. Her dresses were always too short, too long or too tight. Every hairstyle was ugly or not her. Things didn't fit her face. Often times, he'd say mean and insensitive things to put her down and lower her self-esteem.

"You're so stupid! You can't do anything right," was often shouted. Tyrell even went as far as to say, "You wouldn't be nothin without me!"

"What was he talking about? I still didn't actually have him. So what did he mean by that?" she pondered.

"You're getting fat Camille!" he'd cruelly say.

It was true! Camille had gained about eight pounds from the time she first started dating him but she was hardly fat! Tyrell uttered those words so many times that Camille began to feel insecure about her appearance. On a warm sunny day at the beach, a bright, colorful sleeveless sundress and expensive sandals was her preference of attire. Her full figured hips and large breast were by far her best attributes. No one would question the fact that her thighs and triceps needed a little work. Even though, most of the men and women she knew reassured Camille she was no where near being fat, two piece bathing suits were out! The more Tyrell complained, the larger she actually got.

Camille's insecurities mounted as she reflected back to the days when she was a young teenager weighing a slim 120 lbs at 5'7. Everyone use to comment on how slim she was. Her aunt Bessie who lived in Maryland, would use her as an example for her cousin Tanya. Unfortunately, Tanya was constantly battling a weight problem at seventeen.

"Look at your cousin Camille! She's so slim. If you didn't eat so much you'd look like her," Camille's aunt would badger Tanya.

To this day, Camille's cousin still resented her because of it. Embarrassed by her current weight, Camille was afraid to visit her relatives in Maryland.

As the relationship continued, Tyrell's active participation lessened. He never made any plans for them to go anywhere or for them to be alone. Sometimes she felt alone and unwanted while in presence. On a couple of occasions they were uncomfortably accompanied by some of his teammates on dates. Camille felt she was the only one working to keep the relationship going. Tyrell was just there.

In no time, their problems had extended beyond Tyrell, Camille and his friends. His family had now become an issue because they were always nasty and unfriendly toward Camille. More than once, someone in his family called her by his ex-girlfriends' name. Camille wondered if it was done intentionally or if it was because she was still in the picture. The mere site of his mother or one of his aunts sparked a major attitude from Camille.

What made the situation worse was for some unknown reason, Tyrell felt the need to constantly remind Camille how much his family disliked her. At some point during every argument, he'd throw in.

"That's why nobody in my family likes you!"

"Forget your family! I don't care if they like me or not," she'd respond in anger.

The following week, they would be at one of his relatives' homes having dinner and she would unsuccessfully try to pretend she was happy and comfortable. How could she feel happy around them when she knew they didn't like her?

In the fall quarter, Tyrell was accepted to the University of California Los Angeles. Thanks to Camille's efforts, he was also granted financial aid. Tyrell left U.C. Berkeley and moved back to LA where he got an apartment with an ex-high school teammate who was now playing football for U.C.L.A. Coincidentally, one of Camille's mother's friends, who owned a business, had a part-time job available at his office. After turning down the job herself, she insisted her mother's friend hire Tyrell. Tyrell was still in need of money.

Naturally, things should have looked brighter for them but in contrast, things worsened. Their problems escalated when three of his ex-teammates that he felt were not as good, landed spots on professional football teams. He was starting to question weather he'd made the right decision by giving up football. Camille figured Tyrell also held her to blame for pushing him into his decision. More and more, Tyrell resented Camille for helping him. He'd intentionally belittle her to make himself feel bigger and in control. Wet teardrops running down Camille's cheek and a hoarse voice from arguing was an all too familiar event in her life. She should have had a clue something was wrong but she didn't.

There was one bright spot in Camille's life during this time. One day, while she was walking to class, Camille saw a booth with a group of females gathered around it. She curiously approached the booth for clarification.

"Excuse me. Have you ever thought about pledging to a sorority?" a young woman sitting behind the booth asked.

The woman's face was familiar to her. Camille had seen the woman along with her sorority sisters around campus and at a few dances. Pledging had crossed Camille's mind. One of her mother's friends was a doctor and belonged to this sorority. She had her act together. She was always positive and confident. Camille admired her because she was active in the community, just as these young women were. To Camille, this sorority personified strength, togetherness and direction. She wanted to model herself after her mother's friend. Camille may have been having some problems now but she was confident that when the smoke cleared, she'd be a successful woman.

"Yes, I've thought about it," Camille answered.

"We're having a rush meeting tonight in the student union. We're going to tell people what we're looking for and how to pledge. Why don't you come?"

"That sounds good. I'll be there."

As promised, Camille showed up to the meeting. The information she received was positive. This was something she really wanted to do. The professionalism displayed was definitely in the scheme of her life.

Christmas day, as it should have been, was a day to remember. Camille didn't remember this particular Christmas for joyous reasons. She remembered this one because it was when her relationship with Tyrell came to a head. Tyrell decided they would spend Christmas day with his family. What could be more horrible than spending Christmas, which is a day of love, with a group of people she despised. Of course when she arrived at his mother's house she had an attitude. About an hour into their visit, Tyrell angrily pulled her aside and asked her how come she wasn't being friendly.

"It's hard to be friendly toward people you know that don't like you!" she explained.

"I'm tired of you always talking about my family like you're better than they are!" he yelled.

"I'm only repeating what you've told me!" she replied with more of an attitude.

"If you don't want to be here then leave!"

"Fine! I'll leave then! I didn't want to come anyway!"

Later that night, Camille heard a knock at the front door. Looking out of the window, she observed Tyrell's car parked in the driveway with the motor running. Judging by his facial expression, he still appeared upset over what had happened earlier. He was not alone in his anger because she was also still upset her damn self.

"What do you want?" she rudely asked.

"I came to get my stuff!"

"What stuff?" she asked in puzzlement.

"I want my jacket, sweats and all the tee-shirts I let you borrow. That stuff! Where is it?"

Thinking to herself, she thought. "Oh no! If he wants to take his things from my house then he must not have any intentions on coming back."

Suddenly, Tyrell's clothes became an instrument of control. If she gave them up, he wouldn't have a reason to come back. If she kept them, then he'd have to come back later. Maybe by then, he wouldn't be as mad.

"Why do you want your clothes?"

"Just give me my stuff Camille!"

"No! I'm not giving you anything until you tell me why you want them."

Without asking further, Tyrell shoved Camille aside. He then stormed into her room and began ransacking her dresser drawers and closet for his clothes.

"Don't be going through my stuff! What's wrong with you!" she shouted.

Tyrell grabbed a couple of items and then headed out the door. By the time Camille caught up to him he was about to open his car door. Grabbing him by his arm and holding him from getting into his car, she distressfully asked, "Why are you doing this?"

Tyrell's right hand wrapped tightly around her throat and slowly squeezed the breath out of her body like a python. Through her hazy eyes, it appeared he was slowly trying to torture her. Next, she felt a sense of weightlessness before crashing down on the pavement. At first Camille thought she had fallen from a lack of oxygen. It didn't dawn on her she'd just been body slammed to the ground. Camille woke up about two minutes later and found herself lying approximately ten feet away from her conscious position. Blood was grotesquely flowing from a deep cut on her chest. Several deep scratches circled her neck. Camille's entire right side hurt like hell, including her elbow and knee.

When her head finally cleared, Camille felt totally embarrassed. She quickly looked down the street to see if any neighbors were watching. "Oh God please! I hope my dad didn't see it!" she prayed. Camille knew if her father had seen the incident, he would have been terribly upset. Most of all, she didn't want him to pass judgment on Tyrell based on this one incident.

When her vision became clearer, she was surprised to see Tyrell sitting quietly in his car starring at her sprawled out body. Picking herself up, she staggered over to his car.

"Why did you do this to me?" she asked while ejecting tears.

"Get off my car!" he shouted as he pulled out of her driveway. "You brought this mess on yourself."

By the time Tyrell arrived home, he had to have at least four messages on his answering machine from Camille. When she didn't get a return call in the amount of time that she expected, she called again. Camille wasn't exactly sure how many messages she left. Sometimes she left a message and then other times she didn't. After God knows how many attempts, Tyrell finally answered his phone.

"What's wrong with you? Why did you do that?" she asked again.

"I'm tired of you Camille. You ain't nothin. You're always acting childish. It's over!" he firmly stated.

"What did I do?" she repeatedly cried.

Tyrell couldn't give an exact explanation for his discontent. Camille was forced to ponder over their relationship and come up with a reason for herself. As usual, the only flaw she could detect was in Camille.

"I made him trip out. I always make him upset!"

Nothing was settled over the phone Christmas night. Over the next two weeks, Tyrell and Camille heatedly argued about the imperfections in their relationship. Most of her time was spent crying and choking from sorrow while Tyrell yelled.

On January first, their relationship self-destructed. They had not spoken to each other in several days. Camille was not about to start the New Year off in limbo by wondering, "What is the status of our relationship? Where do I stand?" Their telephone conversations were usually cut short because one of them usually hung up in the other's face. A face to face confrontation was the only possible way to get a definite answer. With that in mind, Camille jumped in her car and headed over to Tyrell's apartment.

The apartment complex where Tyrell lived was still reaming with the festive atmosphere of New Years Eve. Front doors to almost every apartment were open. Loud play by play broadcasts of the Rose Bowl football game blasted throughout the complex. Camille casually invited herself inside Tyrell's open apartment. As she entered, she spotted Tyrell, his roommate and his roommate's girlfriend Gina, sitting in the living room playing cards and watching the football game. Camille's sudden appearance ignited an ugly rage in Tyrell.

"What in the hell are you doing here?" he shouted.

"I want to talk to you about us?"

"There is no us!" he screamed. I'm glad you're here cause you have some things here. Take your things and get the hell out!"

Tyrell rose out of his chair and ran into his bedroom. Seconds later, he returned with a handful of clothes belonging to Camille. Camille curiously wondered what he planned to do with her clothes. Tyrell stormed past Camille and then exited through the front door. Taking three quick stutter steps, he twisted his upper body at the waist. Then, he unwound like a shot putter and hurled her clothes over the balcony. Like autumn leaves falling off a tree, Camille's clothes fluttered down into the center courtyard.

"Get out!" he screamed before palming her face with his hands and shoving her over the couch.

"Don't push me!"

Camille's natural reaction was to fight back. She did so by charging him and punching him in the jaw. From that point, the fight was on. Tyrell punched and bounced Camille around the room like a rag doll. She gave it her all but the best she could do was slip in a punch here and there. Her punches ultimately had no effect on Tyrell what so ever. In the end, Camille found herself lying on her back. She fearfully looked up and saw Tyrell sitting on top of her with his fist cocked back and ready to fire. Just in the nick of time, Gina grabbed Tyrell and screamed, "No Tyrell! You're going to kill her!" Catching himself, he lowered his fist and then lifted himself off Camille. From there, he stormed back into his room and slammed the door behind him.

If it weren't for Gina frantically screaming from fright at the top of her lungs and trying to intervene,

Tyrell would have delivered the final deadly punch. As Gina stared down at Camille in horror, Camille could see Gina shaking. Camille was the one who got the hell beat out of her and yet Gina was the one who looked traumatized. Her facial expression alone caused Camille to be ashamed of what she'd become.

Summing it all up, Camille was a loving and caring punching bag who felt like crap! She had very little self-esteem. So much of her energy was consumed by helping Tyrell that she needed someone else to literally help her up off the ground. Camille was a fool.

Gina sympathetically placed her arm around Camille and escorted her out of the apartment. Together they walked into the courtyard and gathered Camille's clothes.

"Are you alright girl?" she asked with care.

"I don't know. My body hurts all over."

"Do you need me to drive you to the police station?" Gina asked.

"The police?"

Not once had Camille ever thought of herself as being the victim of a crime. Filing a police report against a boyfriend who hit her never entered her mind. She didn't see herself as an abused woman. In her mind, other women got abused, not Camille.

Abused women just stood around and got the crap beaten out of them. Camille always fought back. In her opinion, her injuries were never serious enough to be classified as abuse.

As Camille bent down scrounging around for clothes, the actuality of filing a police report against Tyrell became more real. Camille was seriously considering making the report. Was it because her body hurt more than ever? Or, was it because she was embarrassed by Gina's reaction?

"No thank you. I'll drive myself to the police station," Camille told her.

The burden of holding in her emotional and physical pain was too much to carry alone. On the way to the police station, Camille stopped at a phone booth and called home with the intent of spilling her guts to her mother. She knew her mother not only understood what she was going through but she'd unquestionably give Camille some much-needed moral support. Unexpectedly, Camille's older brother Ricky answered the phone. Her brother was only one year older than she was. Ricky was a positive, bright, career oriented young man. The problem was, he could be a hot head, especially when it came to defending his little sister's honor. As a child, Camille would start fights with the neighborhood boys and the moment she'd get behind on points, her big brother would always jump in to defend her. That's why she never told him about her experiences with James. If he had known, he probably would have killed him.

"Ricky, where's Mama?" she asked while sniffing mucus back up into her nostrils.

"She's gone," he answered. Sensing something was wrong, he then asked, "What's wrong with you? Why you crying?"

"Tyrell hit me"

"What!" he shouted. "He needs his butt kicked. I never did like that punk!"

"Tell mom I called. I'll talk to you later," she concluded.

Camille jumped back into her car and headed to where she thought the police station was located. She knew it wasn't far. Camille was not all that familiar with the area and found the police station somewhat difficult to find. Finally, while making a left turn at an intersection, she could see a concrete building with an American flag blowing from a flagpole in front. "That must be it!" she thought to herself as she made the left turn. While parking the car, she questioned herself, "Am I doing the right thing?"

Before exiting her car, Camille flipped down the mirror on her sun visor and checked herself over. Her messed up hair, wrinkled clothes and smeared mascara was consistent with the struggle she'd just went through. Even though she'd just been through hell and her appearance understandably reflected it, there was no way she could enter into a public place looking the way she did. Women with no regard and little respect for themselves were the only ones who got abused. She wanted to make sure no one mistook her for that.

Opening her purse, Camille removed a brush and some cosmetics. Taking a moment, she tidied up her hair, applied fresh lipstick and mascara. At last glance, she was not completely satisfied with her appearance but it was the best she could do under the circumstances.

Camille stepped out of her car, brushed off her clothes and hesitantly walked into the station. The lobby of the station was slightly crowded with neatly dressed people who mainly wanted to report a traffic accident or their car broken into. Camille felt out of place.

New years day was one of the busiest days of the year at the West Los Angeles police station. Domestic violence, loud parties and family disputes were a normality on this special day. Most police officers, like civilians wanted the day off to be with their families. Those who were forced to work were usually not in good spirits. Those who were forced to work at the front desk on this day were twice as unhappy. Camille noticed the desk officers whispering to each other as she entered the station.

"Don't look now, troubles' walking through the door," one officer whispered to another.

"It's gotta be a domestic violence. Her boyfriend or her husband probably beat her butt for the one-hundredth time," the other officer negatively responded.

The two male officers sitting behind the desk immediately took notice of Camille's entrance and drew a conclusion. A torn shirt, messed up hair and a pair of matching bruises on her cheek and chin made it obvious to them she was there to report a crime of a serious and violent nature. That's why the two male officers lowered their heads and quickly walked out of sight. Their departure left only a sole female officer at the desk to handle the incoming problem.

"Hi, may I help you with something ma'am?"

"Yes, I'd like to make a police report," Camille said.

"What kind of report do you want to make?"

"I don't know. I'm not sure what type of report it is," she answered in frustration.

The female officer could see the frustration and pain on Camille's face. The officer could tell that making a police report was a new experience for the young victim but the officer was willing to bet it wasn't the first or the last time something like this would happen.

The officer knew the odds of this woman filing a police report and then actually following through with all of the criminal procedures was slim to none. Still, as a woman and an officer of the law, she felt compelled to help the woman with compassion and concern unlike some male officers.

"Tell me what happened ma'am."

"My boyfriend beat me up!"

"Do you guys live together?"

"No! " Camille answered.

"Do you have any children together?"

"No! Why are you asking these questions? What difference does it make?" Camille asked the officer in frustration.

"It makes a big difference. If you live together or have a child by him then hitting you is a felony crime. Otherwise, it's only a misdemeanor battery with a small bail amount."

Sobbing and partially choking from a lump in her throat, Camille painfully detailed her beating to the officer. The officer stopped Camille several times during her story and asked Camille to elaborate further on each detail.

"Which hand did he hit you with? Was his hand closed in a fist or did he slap you with an open hand? What did he say to you before he hit you?" the officer asked.

"Why do you need to know that?"

Exercising patience, the officer explained, "It's important that I know exactly what happened so when you guys go to court all the details will be documented. The slightest detail might cause him to get off. I want to makes sure he gets what he deserves."

Doubt resurfaced in Camille's mind. She knew Tyrell's actions were wrong and something had to be done about his violent behavior. Was jail the answer? He was already having problems with his life, this would only make things worse. He needed someone to talk to him and tell him he was wrong. Her effort was futile. Maybe if he spoke to an authoritative figure such as a uniformed police officer, he'd listen.

The officer, who appeared to be deeply embroiled in the writing of the report, paused for a moment. Squinting her eyes and moving closer toward Camille, she asked, "What is that long red mark on your shoulder? Did he do that?"

"I don't know?"

Camille turned her head sideways in hopes of getting a look at the undetected scar on her shoulder. A small vein surfaced on the left side of her neck as she strained her head a few inches further to the right than normal.

"That wasn't there before!" she disgustedly answered.

The officer returned her attention back down to the report. Softly whispering out loud to herself, she uttered, "I observed a small laceration on the victim's right shoulder."

Over and over again, the officer took time out from writing her report to comb over Camille's body for further evidence of abuse. The officer's concern for the smallest detail reaffirmed Camille's belief that she was right in her decision to file a police report on Tyrell. To know someone was on her side made her feel comfortable. Also, knowing someone else beside herself viewed his actions as wrong, gave her the inner strength to continue with the report.

Out of Camille's powerful vision, she could see a small group of male officers whispering among themselves and peering at her from a spacious room located to the rear of the desk. The large room contained a multitude of typewriters and computers, which were occupied by female civilian employees. The male officer's actions were typical of most little adult boys who were interested in a woman but didn't have the nerve to approach them.

Whispering, one male officer said to another, "She looks good!"

"Yep, I'd even take her with the bruises."

"Shall I try to put my bid in?" one asked.

"Well, one things' for sure. She's not in a good relationship. Maybe you can hit it before she goes back to him."

"Let me go up there and get a closer look. You never know, it could be a man."

Just when Camille's confidence had risen to its highest level, a male officer returned to the front counter. Quickly glancing at the officer, she involuntarily gave him the "once-over." The officer's neatly groomed hair and mustache, along with his slender build and self-assuring mannerism sparked an immediate physical attraction from Camille. In another time and place, the handsome officer and Camille may have bonded.

Upon meeting her, most men viewed her as beautiful, smart, intelligent and ambitious. Playing the role of a strong goal oriented woman who didn't take any mess was easy for Camille to do. Normally, her dazzling appearance and assertive qualities made her feel cute and special.

As Camille stood in front of the station counter looking helpless, she felt neither cute nor special. Instead, she felt vulnerable. She felt like she was standing naked for all the world to see what was underneath her coat of armor. In another setting, she may have lured the officer toward her with a semi-flirtatious smile but this time she was so embarrassed by her visible injuries that she refused to look up. How could she play the tough role with anyone who had seen her in such a vulnerable state?

"Okay ma'am," the female officer said as she scooted the report in front of Camille. "I need you to sign your name on the line."

After signing the report, Camille asked, "So what happens now?"

"Now we wait for the detectives to call you."

Naively thinking justice would be swift, Camille in frustration, said, "You mean you're not going to go over there and arrest him?"

"No, because it's only a misdemeanor and you're not there. If you had called us from there then we might have arrested him."

"So what should I do?"

"Don't talk to him and make sure you stay away from him. If he hit you once, he'll hit you a second time. Trust me. It'll only get worse!" the officer sincerely answered while tearing off the back of the report. "This yellow sheet is your copy of the report, hold on to it."

Camille felt as though she'd just won a moral victory after walking out of the police station proudly holding her copy of the police report. It was as if her copy of the report was a certificate of merit, proof she'd accomplished an incredible feat. Camille had just slew the evil dragon!

Immediately after arriving home, she anxiously looked around the house for her mother. To Camille's surprise, the house was empty. Eagerly in need of a boost, she picked up the phone and scheduled a hair and nail appointment at the hair salon. She felt an absolute need to boost her appearance to her confidence level. The only bad thing about making a hair appointment on an afternoon following a holiday was she couldn't get an appointment until eight. This meant she wouldn't actually see the beautician until nine. There was no doubt in her mind that her hair wouldn't be finished until midnight. Regardless, she did it.

When Camille arrived home after her appointment, she again looked around the house for her support. Creeping into her mother's room, Camille became disheartened when she observed her mother curled up and fast asleep. That meant she was going to have to carry her burden until morning.

The next morning, Camille rose from her bed bright and early to the grinding sound of Slim Fast mixing in the blender. Next to the blender stood Camille's moral support, her confidant, her mother.

"Good morning Mom!"

Good morning Camille," she answered in a solemn tone. "I heard that you had a problem with Tyrell yesterday."

"Yeah. . . How did you know?"

"Your brother told me. Why did you have to get your brother involved? What happens between you and Tyrell is your business, not his!"

"What are you talking about? I didn't get him involved in anything," Camille answered.

Raising her tone of voice a bit, she said, "Yes you did! After he spoke to you on the phone yesterday, he and some of his friends tried to find Tyrell's apartment so they could beat him up. What if he had gone over there, beat him up and then got arrested and went to jail? How would you have felt?"

"I didn't ask him to go over there!"

"He went over there because he was worried about you. Nobody knew where you were. Where did you go?"

"I went to the police station to make a police report."

A look of surprise popped on her mother's face. "The police station?" she asked with astonishment. "Why did you go to the police? How come you didn't just come home?"

Camille was puzzled. This was not the support she'd hope to get. "What in the hell was going on? Was my mother siding with Tyrell? Did she disapprove of me filing a police report against him?" Camille thought.

"I went to the police because he hit me! He's not supposed to hit me!" she said.

As usual, her mother was calm and poised. "You're absolutely right, he's not suppose to put his hands on you. I'm not upset with you because you made a police report. I'm just concerned with how it's going to affect you."

"What do you mean?"

"I mean, can you live with the fact your decision may cause him to go to jail? I know you Camille. You're soft hearted and caring. You're not

170

hard enough to send him to jail and not feel guilty about it."

"Yes I am!" Camille shot back. "He's going to pay for what he did to me!"

Her mother's opinion was always a much-valued commodity. Even though Camille didn't quite agree with her on this issue, her words of wisdom were definitely something to consider, particularly the part about wrongfully getting her brother involved in the her mess. She understood why her mother got upset with her for telling Ricky what happened. In actuality, she was right. Camille intentionally involved Ricky. Camille knew he would get mad and then try to do something to Tyrell. Deep down, Camille wanted him to go over to Tyrell's apartment and give him what he deserved.

The female officer's words of wisdom were also something to seriously consider, "If he hit you once, he'll hit you again. . ." Camille was convinced Tyrell had a serious problem. She honestly believed he would do it again if she immediately went back to him. Camille promised herself she wouldn't call him again.

Later that morning, Camille found her brother sitting in front of the television set talking on the telephone. Ricky glanced up and immediately got off the phone with whomever he was talking to, something Tyrell could never do.

"What's up Camille?" he asked with concern.

"I want to talk to you."

"Don't worry, me and my buddies are gonna take care of that sissy for you. Yesterday, we tried to find his apartment but we couldn't. Where does he live?" her brother asked.

"Don't worry about it Ricky. I went to the police and made a police report. They'll take care of it."

"You sure? We still can handle it for you if you want?"

"I'm sure. I got it under control," she assured him.

Camille assured Ricky she had everything under control but did she really? Camille couldn't help thinking about what her mother had told her. "Was I making the right decision? After all, Tyrell was young and had expressed interest in politics as well as law enforcement. Was it really fair for him to suffer for the rest of his life for something he did when he was young? Probably not," she concluded.

A whole week and a half past by and Camille still hadn't heard from Tyrell nor a police detective. In a week, she would begin pledging on campus. There wouldn't be any room in her already busy schedule for her to pledge, attend classes and go to court. With those excuses firmly embedded in Camille's mind, she went back to the police station to speak to a detective.

As she walked into the station for a second time, why did she have to see the same female officer who so patiently took her report?

Camille felt badly. "Why couldn't I have come to the station when she was off or at lunch?"

"Don't tell me you're here to drop the charges?" the female officer said in disgust.

"I have no choice but to drop them. I have a busy schedule," Camille explained.

"Are you sure you want to do this?" she asked. "Is he making you do this?"

"No. I'm doing this on my own. He doesn't even know I was down here. I haven't spoken to him since it happened."

"I knew you'd be back. I could see it in your eyes. You haven't had enough yet. It won't be until he puts you in the hospital until you get enough," the officer said with some resentment. Then, she shook her head in dismay and concluded, "I hope you're not sorry."

From there, she sent Camille down the hall to the detective area. Camille was then introduced to a male detective who stood over her and questioned her as if she was a suspect. Drilling questions at Camille, he asked, "Why are you dropping charges?"

"I have a lot of things to do so I can't go to court," she answered.

"Is he making you do it?"

"No."

"Is he threatening you?"

"No!"

"Are you afraid of him?"

"No!"

"Is his family threatening you?"

"No!"

"Don't you know he'll do it again!" he yelled.

Confused by the questioning, Camille answered. "No! I mean yes. I mean I'm not going back to him."

"If you're not going back then why are you dropping the charges? Is he making you?" he asked.

Camille firmly stayed with her decision, even if it meant Tyrell was going to skate on this one. As she walked out of the station, the female police officer and the detective created an air of disappointment that filled the lobby. Despite their obvious disappointment, Camille felt confident that she was doing what had to be done. She convinced herself that by dropping the charges, she was making a decision to move on with her life. She didn't want to dwell on the pass.

James hurt Camille but she easily dismissed that phase of her life as a virtue of youth. With James, she really didn't know any better. She was naively lured into his web by the attention he gave her. Camille's situation with Tyrell was totally different.

No matter how hard she tried to move on, there wasn't any way she could shake the devastating psychological effects she suffered from this relationship. Her break-up with Tyrell was far more damaging than any relationship she'd had. Tyrell was supposed to be a good friend first and foremost. Because of that, Camille put extra effort into being a good, supportive friend to him. She opened her heart to him and painfully showed him her inhibited emotions. Camille was what a true friend should be. She did everything in her power to help Tyrell help himself.

Obviously that wasn't enough. Subconsciously, she was thinking her failed relationship meant she had failed as a person or perhaps she wasn't a good enough person to keep him.

"Maybe it doesn't pay to be honest, kind and sincere in a relationship? Maybe I shouldn't go into another one whole heartedly?"

YOU NEVER KNOW A GOOD
THING UNTIL IT'S GONE

The following week, school and pledging occupied Camille's time. There was literally nothing else in her life, including no Tyrell. During her many weeks of pledging, Tyrell neither called nor came by. Ironically, he had no idea she was about to become his sorority sister.

Three weeks after she had crossed over from an individual to a Greek, Camille and her sorors performed at a Greek step show. The buzzing atmosphere of the step contest was electrifying and pridy. After they performed on stage, Camille and her sorors filed off stage. They marched into the stands to take a seat but none were available. Parading down the aisles in single file, they were lead to a section already occupied by their fraternity big brothers. Each soror took a seat on a fraternity brother's lap.

It was only proper Camille knew the name of the person whose lap she was sitting on. Mark was his name. He was very nice and mannerly as well as good looking. Through casual conversation, Camille found out he lived and went to school seventy-five miles away in San Bernardino County. After the show, Camille and Mark said good-bye and went their separate way. That was until they saw one another the next day at a picnic. This time they had the opportunity to chat in depth. Mark turned out to be a really intelligent and sincere person. He was worthy of having Camille's phone number as a friend only! Even though he possessed all the qualities she was looking for in a man, there wasn't any immediate animal magnetism jumping off between them. At least not for Camille anyway.

Why was it always like that? When Camille and her girlfriends got together and discussed men, they always said they wanted their prince charming to be someone who was nice, polite, good looking, sincere and nicely built. For some weird reason, when that person stood in their faces and smiled, they thought he was goofy, a nerd or just not interesting. Camille's prince charming was staring her in the face and she didn't know it or maybe she didn't know how to deal with it.

After their first date, Camille received flowers and a card. The second, candy and a card. Camille's hair was blown back by Mark's kindness and good-hearted nature. Before she knew it, they were seeing one another every weekend. It seemed like every weekend, he was either driving down to LA to see her or Mark would come down to L.A., pick her up and then take Camille to San Bernardino. The relationship was good. Mark and Camille did some of everything together including movies, dinner, amusement parks, plays, poetry readings; you name it they did it.

Every time she saw him, he would slip a card of endearment in her purse. Sometimes he'd pretend he left something in her room. Then he would go back inside and leave a card on Camille's dresser for her to find after he was gone. In the course of a year, Mark must have left at least thirty cards for Camille to find. They seldom argued. If they did, the arguments were so small and insignificant Camille didn't remember them.

A substantial amount of their time was spent attending sorority and fraternity functions. Everyone knew Camille and Mark as a couple. It almost became impossible for anyone to mention one without the other. They were like the Prince Charles and Princess Diane of the Greek world. What made the situation more interesting were Mark and her ex-boyfriend Tyrell belonged to the same fraternity. Camille shouldn't have given it a second thought, especially since Tyrell was not all that involved in Greek functions. The odds of them running into each other were slim. It was a small world and word traveled through the grapevine very quickly. It really shouldn't have mattered. Camille hadn't spoken to Tyrell in over four months and without question, their relationship was over.

Instead of letting Mark find out through the grapevine that she had dated one of his fraternity brothers, out of courtesy, Camille decided to break it down to him herself. Leaving out the descriptive details, she explained that she and Tyrell dated and departed on bad terms. Mark didn't have a problem with it.

Ironically, two weeks later, Camille and Mark were at Greek show when Camille sensed a pair of eyes penetrating her back. The peering eyes belonged to an unknown male who was standing on the second level of the college auditorium. When she looked up, he beckoned for her to come up to where he was standing. Squinting her eyes, Camille tried to focus on the guy. She tried to figure out who he was and why he wanted her to come up to where he was. It was more than obvious she was with Mark.

It only took Camille a few seconds before she realized that it was Tyrell who was standing up there watching her every move. Camille immediately acknowledged his presence by frowning and shaking her head no. Camille was through with Tyrell. She had nothing to say to him. Camille then turned back around and gave Mark her undivided attention.

"The nerve of that guy! I hadn't seen or heard from him in months. Does he really expect me to leave Mark and come see what he wants?"

A couple of nights later, Camille and Mark were romantically curled up in her room watching a movie on video when their peaceful moment was abruptly interrupted by a phone call. This was strange because most of her friends were either sleep at this hour or somewhere with their boyfriends.

"Who could be calling me at this time of night?" she thought.

"Hi Camille. How are you?" the caller asked.

"I'm fine. . . Who is this?"

"This is Tyrell."

At the sound of his voice, Camille's heart sunk to the pit of her stomach. Talk about bad timing. Tyrell couldn't have picked a worse time if he had planned it. There was no way she could talk to him right there and then with Mark sitting beside her. It didn't matter anyway because she didn't have anything to say to him.

"Well I'm busy right now. I'll talk to you later. Bye!" **CLICK!**

No sooner than she hung up, the phone rang again. "Damn! Who's this calling me now?" she pondered.

"Hello?"

"Can you come outside?" Tyrell asked.

Irritated, she asked, "For what?"

"I'm calling you from outside your house on my cellular phone. I just want to talk to you for a minute," he persistently tried to convince her.

"No! Bye!" **CLICK!**

RING! RING! RING!

"Oh please God, don't let that be Tyrell again!"

RING! RING! RING!

Tyrell was creating an awkward situation for Camille. She was embarrassed. Mark, who had been sitting in front of the television pretending not to hear the conversation, was now moving around restlessly on the couch. Camille started not to answer the phone but she knew how persistent Tyrell could be. He'd probably let the phone ring all night if he had to.

Picking up the phone, she asked, "What do you want?"

"I just want you to know that I'm sorry for all the things I did to you. I was going through a lot."

"It's too late for that now!" **CLICK!**

RING!

"What!" Camille shouted into the phone.

"I know that I was wrong. . ."

"Look! Stop calling here. If you want to talk about it, I'll call you tomorrow." **CLICK!**

RING!

"Yes!"

Camille's refusal to speak with Tyrell seemed to bring about a tone of desperation in his voice. "Tell your friend to step out. I want to talk to him!" he yelled in frustration.

"Why are you wanting to talk to me now? It's too late for that now! Don't call me anymore tonight or I'm going to call the police!" **CLICK!**

Camille's escapade with Tyrell was confusing and nerve rattling. What troubled her the most was Mark having to uncomfortably suffer while she and Tyrell argued. Camille could only imagine what he must have been thinking. Whatever it was, it couldn't be good. She felt a need to explain.

"I'm sorry about that honey. That was Tyrell, he's trippin."

"I figured it was him," Mark said as he stood up and put his jacket on.

"Where you going?"

"I'm leaving. It's obvious you guys need to straighten this out. Call me when you've worked it out."

Holding onto his arm, Camille painfully replied, "No! I don't want you to leave. There's nothing to work out! He's not in my life anymore, you are!"

"I don't think he knows that. Maybe you should call him back and tell him and then call me later," he concluded.

"I don't want to call him back," she whined. "Don't leave, stay!"

The effort she put into keeping Mark at bay was useless. Mark gently gave Camille a kiss on the cheek and then walked out the door. Camille's big fear was that he would never return. In any case, there was nothing she could do to stop him. Her feelings were deeply hurt by this sudden twist of irony. Camille had spent several long, depressing and heartbroken months trying to forget everything about Tyrell. Finally, when she'd accomplished her goal and found someone else, he popped back up. Tyrell was putting a damper back in her life.

"How come he couldn't just go away?. . . I have no intentions of calling him back tonight or ever again!"

RING! RING.

"This better not be him!" she said to herself. "Hello!" she shouted in anger.

"Don't hang up Camille," Tyrell pleaded. "I just want to apologize."

"There's no need to apologize Tyrell. That was then. I've moved on," Camille coldly responded.

"I'd like to see you Camille. How about going to a movie with me?"

"No thanks. I don't see any reason for us to go out. There's nothing left! Everything we had together was destroyed."

"That's not true Camille. I'm different now. I've learned a lot in the months we were apart."

"It's too late!" **CLICK!**

Tyrell didn't call back again that night but every now and then he'd call and leave Camille a thoughtful or apologetic message on her answering machine. From that day on, Tyrell overtly made his presence known by going to every Greek function around, something he never would do. His resurgence triggered uneasiness, confession and doubt in Camille's mind. Kelvin, James and Tyrell all ended up being assholes despite starting off as sweethearts like Mark. Camille psyched herself into believing, "all good things must come to an end," at least when it comes to men.

"How long will it be before Mark starts acting like a jerk? How long will it be before he begins to put me down and then try to control me like all the rest? When will I cry because of something he says?" she thought. "It's only a matter of time before Mark breaks my heart like the others. Why should I give all of myself to him and the relationship when I know it's not going to last?"

All of a sudden, Camille started feeling like Mark was suffocating her with his presence. Their daily phone conversations combined with seeing one another every weekend became tiresome. Not only did she need some space, a $400 a month phone bill was ridiculous! The amount of the bill became so large Camille had to make arrangements with the telephone company to pay her bill in installments. Eventually, her deficit continued to compound until she could no longer keep up with her payments. Subsequently, her phone and lifeline to Mark was cut off.

The only way Mark could reach Camille was by calling her mother's phone. Camille couldn't really explain it, but for no apparent reason, she would ask her mother to tell Mark that she wasn't home or she was asleep. Then, she wouldn't call him back until a week later. When she did finally call him back, Mark would be belligerent, rude and a little hostile.

Sometimes they would viciously argue. Mark was extremely upset about Camille's new and sudden lackadaisical attitude.

"Why didn't you call me back?" he'd shout.

"I was busy. Don't yell at me!"

"You ain't that damn busy where you can't call me back for a week! You've sure got plenty of time to hang out on the weekends with your girlfriends!"

"So what! You're just mad cause I ain't up under you all the time. All you want to do is control me!"

"Control you? Why in the hell would I want to control you? You ain't nothing to control!"

"Shut the hell up Mark! You ain't nothin!" Camille would often scream.

Camille could remember a time when she and Mark never argued or disagreed. Now, all they did was argue and nothing ever got solved. In the beginning, if ever there were a misunderstanding, they would quickly solve it by compromising. Unfortunately, those days seemed to be over.

"Camille, you're pushing Mark away," her mother once advised her.

"Whatever Mom!" she responded.

Mother was right. Although that wasn't Camille's intentions, she was letting her personal problems affect her relationship. Slowly but surely, she was subconsciously pushing Mark out of her life. Camille's inexcusable antics continued to go on for about three months. The final back breaker came when she forgot to call Mark on his birthday.

Three days later, Camille received a card from Mark. Receiving a letter from him wasn't all that strange because he'd often use cards as a way to express feelings of admiration. The inscription on the outside of the card read, *"**The only thing that matters is I love you.**"*

The inside of the card also contained a personal hand written note from him.

*"**Camille, I know the past couple of months have been hectic, busy and sometimes frustrating for both of us. I know there have been times when I've made a big deal over the smallest things but that's only because I love you and it's so very hard to be away from the most beautiful thing in my life, and that's you.***

I'm sorry Camille. Please forgive me and try to understand you are such an important part of my life that the very thought of losing you is going to hurt me more than I can bare. Just remember Camille, although I may not be with you in the flesh, my spirit will always be with you and

you will always be in my heart forever. I love you
Camille, Mark.

"What kind of stuff is this? What did he mean by, Losing you is going to hurt"?

Camille wondered why Mark was apologizing. He never did anything she knew which warranted an apology. Camille knew he had been upset about not seeing her but that wasn't a big deal.

"Why was he tripping so hard over such a little incident? Something is definitely wrong!"

Camille was confused because she never told him that he'd lost her. She was still there for him. Maybe not lately but she felt she hadn't gone anywhere. Although it might not have appeared so, her heart still belonged to Mark. Over all, she was happy with Mark. Camille didn't see a need to seek any type of gratification from another man what so ever. Camille was unhappy with herself! That was the problem. She distanced herself from Mark solely out of frustration with herself.

Camille walked into the other part of the house to use her mother's phone. She had to think hard to remember Mark's telephone number. His phone number was programmed into her phone so all she had to do was push a button and the phone would automatically dial the number for her. Not speaking to

188

him in a while, combined with the confusion generated by the card caused Mark's phone number to fade out of her memory.

Just before she picked up the phone to dial, her mother briskly walked up to her with a card in her hand. With a big smile she joyfully said, "Look Camille. Look what Mark sent me through the mail!"

Removing the card from her mother's hand, Camille curiously opened the card.

"Thank you Mom for all you've done for me in the last year. I can't thank you enough for all of your support. You've been like my mother. Thank you, Mark."

"Aw. . . Mark is so sweet! He's such a nice and thoughtful person Camille," her mother said as she grinned from ear to ear.

Camille's mother perceived the card as an innocent act of gratitude. Camille didn't see it that way. She sensed something was wrong. Of course, the only way she could find out the truth was by making the phone call which she had attempted to do. On her second attempt at dialing Mark's number, Camille got a ring to a number she hoped was his.

RING! RING! RING!

She impatiently tapped her foot on the floor and wiggled her fingers at the anticipation of finding out the true meaning and reason behind the card.

"Hello!" a jubilant Mark answered.

In the background, Camille could hear lots of pots and pans rattling around. She also heard the opening and closing of cabinets and drawers. There was no doubt the noise was coming from the kitchen. She naturally assumed Mark was attempting to cook lunch or trying to wash dishes.

"Hi Mark. This is Camille."

Mark paused for a moment as if he wanted to say, "What are you doing calling here? How did you get my number?" Instead, he politely responded, "Hi Camille. How are you?"

"I'm fine. I got the card you sent me."

Camille left it at that. She was hoping he would voluntarily fill in the gap he'd created in her mind.

"I was wondering when you'd get it and if you'd call me once you did."

His procrastination was starting to piss Camille off, which was easy to do at this period of her life.

"I don't understand why you wrote that stuff on the card? I never told you I didn't want to see you again!"

Mark again paused and then took a deep breath before asking, "Look, um. . . Can I call you back later? Now is not a good time for us to talk."

"What do you mean now is not a good time?" she furiously shouted. "I'm not getting off the phone until I get an answer from you!"

"Okay. I'll give you an answer," he calmly stated. "But. . ."

Suddenly Marks low, calm voice was interrupted by another loud, high-pitched voice rang out from a distance. Camille could tell the voice was coming from another room inside of his house.

"Mark!" the female voice shouted. "Where do you keep your big pots and pans at? I can't find any!"

Covering the phone with his hand, he shouted, "Look down underneath the counter. There should be one under there."

"Oh my God! Another woman, in my house, cooking in my kitchen for my man! What in the hell is going on?"

Suddenly, an indescribable feeling rushed over Camille? She was totally breath taken and slightly nauseated. A sharp pain pierced her chest and her head throbbed. It was almost as if a mallet of awareness had falling on her.

Suddenly, the meaning of the card became clear. The message was not as she had thought. Mark was not under the impression she was leaving him. Mark was politely telling Camille that he was leaving her.

During all the many times Camille had deliberately avoided him, not once did it ever occur to her that one day he would become tired of her mess and leave. She always figured he'd be there for her no matter what she said or did. For some strange reason, Camille thought after her clouds of frustration and confusion was gone, Mark would be waiting for her with open arms. She figured he'd weather the storm because he loved her. She was wrong!

Camille figured there still could be some remote chance of hope. She was hoping Mark would say, "That was my cousin." Clearing her throat and summoning up some vocal strength, Camille asked, "Who's that?"

"I love you Camille so I'm going to be honest. I can't deal with you anymore. I've tried to be understanding but I want someone who wants to be with me and in my company. I've tried to be patient and wait till you came back around but I can't any longer. You've hurt me and the best way for me to get over you is not to see you anymore."

Tears streamed from Camille's eyes and her larynx clogged with fluid as she sorrowfully said, "I love you Mark. I'm sorry! I'll change! I promise."

"I'm sorry Camille it's too late now! Bye," he coldly concluded. **CLICK!**

All afternoon, Camille relentlessly attempted to contact Mark again. The phone line remained busy. Not just for the afternoon but for days. Whenever she'd get through, all Camille managed to get was Mark's answering machine. Mark repeatedly failed to return Camille's calls. It was more than obvious Mark was completely through with Camille.

Later on, through the grapevine, Camille found out that some of her friends had seen Mark in public with this other woman about a month prior to her getting the card. What made Camille's heartburn worse was that she casually knew the woman from Greek functions. This last bit of news made her heart all the more bitter toward life in general. There was a special emphasis on men. Camille wanted to get even.

Camille's heart was completely wrecked and shattered. She repeatedly thought of Mark and how deep down, they were really looking for the same things in a relationship. It was hard for Camille to come to grips with the fact that she got exactly what she asked for. Unfortunately, she let it slip away.

Camille couldn't help but wonder if there still wasn't something she could do to win Mark's heart back. She already tried crying and pleading. Nothing worked.

"What else could I have done? Should I have fought for my man instead of giving up without a fight?"

TILL DEATH DO US PART
(OFFICER MC INTOSH)

It was about one o'clock in the morning and Loretta's husband still hadn't made it home from work yet. What possible reason could there be for his tardiness other than another woman? Why else would it take a no good man nine hours to get home from work. Two years ago, her husband's adultery was not so obvious and blatant. Initially, it began with an hour of unaccountable time. From there came his anonymous phone calls and the hang-ups in her face. Now, he was mysteriously disappearing from home for hours at a time without a good explanation. What was a woman to do in her circumstance? Give up and run? Or stand up and fight for what she felt was hers?

Ten years ago, when Loretta's relationship consisted of only she and her husband, she probably would have fled from her relationship. But now, it involved two young children, a house, numerous bills, bonds, retirements etc. There were just too many variables in her relationship to just give up and start over again. Perhaps, she could put more effort into salvaging her relationship by proving her love and dedication to her husband? What could she do? She wondered.

Suddenly, the sound of a car door being slammed caught Loretta's attention. Running to the front window, she quickly moved the curtains aside and took a peek from her window in anticipation of seeing her husband walking toward the house. Instead, she saw one of her neighbors barefoot in pajamas scurrying from his car to his home on his tiptoes.

The rollers in her hair and the blue silk nightgown she was wearing clearly showed Loretta was ready for bed. She had put the children to bed hours ago but the absence of her husband would not allow her to fall asleep. This was certainly no way for a woman to live. Her life was slowly unraveling before her eyes. Her productivity at work was decreasing while her use of sick time increased. All this was due to her constantly losing sleep and concentration over the whereabouts of her husband. Seventy percent of her thoughts were preoccupied by wondering where her husband was, who he was with and what disease he might bring home to her. At her going rate, she wasn't going to have a job or her insanity much longer which would make her even more dependent on her husband than she already was.

Officer McIntosh and Estrada gave a sigh of relief as they plopped into their patrol car. Their minds were exhausted from having just booked two uncooperative suspects and writing a long detailed report explaining and rationalizing their every move.

Officer McIntosh, who was busy writing the night's events down on his daily log, paused for a moment and said, "Boy! I'm glad we got that junk out of the way!"

"I heard that!"

Upon completing his paper work, McIntosh carefully placed his metal report box underneath his seat and then pressed the clear button on the computer. **BEEP! BEEP! BEEP!** they heard on the radio. "Three Adam Fifteen, handle a shooting in progress in front of 1145 W. 43rd Dr. Approximately ten shots heard and a male is down at the location."

"Three Adam Fifteen roger!" officer McIntosh acknowledged over the radio with excitement.

"Three Adam Fifteen handle code 3," the dispatcher concluded in her broadcast.

The officers' blood and adrenaline began to pump with each passing block they sped past. At last, this was what they lived for and expected to encounter. Reaching down, Officer Estrada flipped a switch, which activated the patrol car's lights and siren. Both officers rolled up their windows so the sound of the siren wouldn't drown out any additional information being broadcasted.

"Three Adam one, show us backing Adam Fifteen on the shooting call!"

"Here we go baby! This is it!" Estrada yelled as the patrol car sped through intersections.

"I bet one of the Rollin Forty Crips got capped. That's their neighborhood. I bet it's probably K-Dog. He's due to be killed."

"And there's supposed to be a gang truce!" Estrada snickered.

As soon as the officers pulled up near 1146, they saw a well dressed, middle-aged man sprawled out on the front lawn of the residence. Exiting the car and cautiously approaching the victim, the first thing they noticed was they were wrong in their suspicions. Their first observations said the shooting was not gang related but in their minds, it was still too early to tell.

On the ground next to the man's body were approximately ten empty bullet casings. It was obvious this was not a drive-by shooting. Whoever shot him got in real close and personal. It was also obvious that whoever shot him wanted him dead.

"He's not a Crip. He's an average working citizen," Estrada said with a puzzled look on his face.

"Maybe not. It could be dope related. Who knows, he could have gotten robbed while trying to by some dope."

The officers bent down at the waist and looked closely at the victim whose mouth was open and his eye-balls rolling back into his head. Officer Estrada roughly used his boot to kick the victim's shoes in an attempt to help him regain consciousness. After several attempts, the victim shook his head and tried to speak to the officers.

Yelling and speaking slowly, officer McIntosh spoke to the victim as if the victim were hard of hearing. "Sir. . . Who shot you?"

Lifting up his bloody arm, the victim pointed west and in a faint breathy voice, he answered, "Down there. . ."

"The person who shot you is down there?" McIntosh asked in clarification.

"I live down there," the man whispered.

"What's your address?"

"1135 W. 43rd Dr. . . My wife. . . My wife. . ."

"You want us to go down there and tell your wife you've been shot?"

"No. . . My wife. . . My wife. She stabbed me and then shot me," the man answered.

As if the officers were playing charades, both in unison yelled, "Oh!. . . Your wife shot you!"

Slapping his hand against his forehead, McIntosh replied, "Geez, why didn't I think of that? The wife did it."

Stomping a foot against the ground, Estrada whimpered, "Damn, this is just another super, giant, colossal domestic violence call!"

"Hang in there buddy. An ambulance will be here real soon," McIntosh told the victim.

In the near distance, the officers could hear a rumbling engine and siren of an ambulance coming nearer. They were relieved to finally see Rescue Ambulance #23 arrive at the scene. Even though the officers didn't really give a darn about the victim, it was still somewhat disturbing for them to helplessly watch a bullet riddled victim die in anguish. As a patrol officer with minimal first aid training, there was little they could do to save the victim's life.

Casually, two paramedics stepped out of the white and red ambulance. Both carried large gray plastic cases containing medical supplies. It would seem under the urgent life or death circumstances, the paramedics would have rushed over to the ailing victim who was fighting death. On the contrary, both paramedics yawned and then stretched before stopping to exchange hand shakes and greetings with the police officers.

"Did we wake you guys?" Estrada asked.

"Not really. It's been a busy night for us. How about you guys? You been busy?"

"We've only been on for about an hour and so far this is the second domestic violence call we've handled."

"This is not a robbery?"

"Nope. His wife shot him and stabbed him."

"Which came first, the chicken or the egg, or shall I say the knife or the gun?" one paramedic joked.

"He must have gotten busted with another woman."

Back to the business at hand, the paramedics moved over to their patient and protected themselves by cover their hands with thick blue latex gloves. Using a pair of scissors, they snipped off his shirt and pants. Then they roughly used their fingers to poke at any hole or mark on the man's body resembling a gunshot or stab wound. Their street-side manners cause the victim to moan and groan in agony.

Turning to the officers, one of the paramedics said, "It looks like he was stabbed once in the stomach and shot three times in the chest."

"Shot three times hum. . .?" McIntosh mumbled. "Looks like he was either blessed, lucky or his wife needs glasses."

"Three times out of ten is not good but if you count the stab wound that makes it four out of eleven tries," Estrada added.

"The stab wound is what will probably kill him," the paramedic said while kneeling and attending to the victim.

"Is he going to make it?"

"Most likely. He's stable. What are you guys gonna do?"

"Well, I guess we're gonna go over to his house and arrest his wife for attempted murder. Hopefully we won't have to kill her."

The two officers loaded themselves into their patrol car and slowly drove westbound toward the suspect's home. The house was only a half block away from the crime scene. The suspect's home was the only house on the block with a porch light on. A glowing light from a television set illuminated the living room. It was as if the suspect was still waiting for her husband to come home. Unknown to the officers, their suspect was a middle-aged working mother of two. As far as they were concerned, she could be a dangerous, barricaded suspect, as dangerous as any other person who has tried to commit murder.

"Three Adam Fifteen, can I get four additional units and an air-unit to my location for an attempt murder suspect?" McIntosh requested.

Minutes later, a police helicopter hovered above while a half-dozen patrol officers swarmed about and strategically positioned themselves around the residence with their guns drawn. Once everyone was in position, McIntosh reminded his partner about the situation they were facing.

"Remember, she has already tried to kill her husband for whatever reasons. As far as she knows, he's dead. She may feel like she has nothing to loose by killing us."

Moving closely along the wall of the house, the officers carefully approached the front door, which they found to be tightly encompassed by a black iron security door. Behind the barred door was a closed wooden door. McIntosh took a position next to the security door while his partner took cover behind a concrete pillar supporting the front porch. McIntosh banged on the door with authority and yelled, "Open up! It's the police!"

Tension began to build when the woman did not come to the door right away. The officers started thinking the worst, she was going to kill herself and anyone in there with her. McIntosh figured the wife was also probably think the worst, the police want to kill her for killing her husband.

"Open up! It's the police! We are not going to hurt you. We know you shot your husband but he's not dead!"

"What do you mean he's not dead?" the woman shouted from inside.

"He's not dead. You're a bad shot. He's in bad shape but he's going to make it."

The woman's voice sounded like she was crying and stressed. "You're only saying that because you want me to come outside so you guys can shoot me."

"We don't want to shoot you. We just wanna talk."

"If you wanna talk then why are there so many of you and why are you hiding behind the door? You're afraid of me aren't you?"

With a smirk, McIntosh replied, "Gee. . . you just tried to shoot your husband ten times. I'd have to say I'm just a little terrified. I don't know, maybe it's just me."

"I don't like you. You have a smart mouth!"

"I'm sorry ma'am but I don't understand why you had to shoot him. What could he have done for you to shoot him?"

The officer's comment caused the woman to fling open the front door in anger. Only the security door came between the officer and the woman. Through the door, McIntosh could plainly see the woman's eyes, nose and lips were swollen. Her blue silk nightgown was spotted with blood that dripped from her face and then down the front of her gown. Half of her hair was still in rollers while the other part hung wildly down around her shoulders.

"Look at my face! Can you see what he did to me! Why are you here trying to arrest me when you see what he did," the woman hysterically shouted.

"We're not here to arrest you ma'am. We just wanna talk. That's all. We want you to come with us to the station so you can explain yourself."

"Why don't you take my husband down to the station and have him explain himself?"

"Well, I would but he's breathing through a tube right now. He can't say much."

"You're a jerk!"

"People keep telling me that. Hum. . . I wonder why? So are you coming or not! I don't have all day. I've gotta eat. "

Keys jiggled and locks turned as the woman gave up. McIntosh and Estrada quickly stepped through the doorway and handcuffed the woman. Once she was cuffed, Estrada walked around the house to see if anyone else was inside. In one of the bedrooms he found two children still sound asleep. Returning to the front, he told his partner about his findings.

"What? Ma'am you have children?"

"Yes," she sadly replied.

"That's a damn shame. Didn't you think about them when you did this?"

"Did he think about the kids when he did this to me? All I did was ask him why he was so late coming home. He had no right to slap me, call me a bitch and start hitting me. All I did was defend myself by grabbing a knife and stabbing him in his stomach. I was so mad that I stuck the butcher's knife into his stomach as far as I could. I tried to make it come out of his back."

Officer McIntosh and Estrada's mouths hung open in the disbelief of the woman's spontaneous confession. "So how did he wind up getting shot a block away?"

"After I stabbed him, he ran out the house. I was so angry I grabbed my gun from under our bed and chased him down the street. At first I couldn't catch him but he finally collapsed from the stab wound. And then I got his ass!" she proudly boosted.

"Did it ever occur to you to call the police?"

"You guys wouldn't have done nothin! He would have only got a slap on the wrist."

"Well now he gets the house, the kids and a new girlfriend. While you're getting felt up in the penitentiary, he'll be knocking boots with another woman in your house and neglecting your kids. That's if he doesn't die tonight," McIntosh joked with anger.

His partner shook his head with a smile. "Damn! partner you're crazy." McIntosh then called another pair of officers into the house to wake up the children and cart them off to Juvenile Hall while he and his partner transported the woman to the station for booking. The officers rolled their eyes at the suspect with disgust and hatred. They couldn't understand how a mother could get so wrapped into her relationship with her husband and forsake her children.

Grabbing the woman by the arm, McIntosh said, "Come on lady, lets go!"

"Wait! Where are my children going?"

"Juvenile Hall!"

"Can I at least put on a robe and slip on some shoes?" she requested.

"If what you're wearing was good enough to do a drive-by shooting in then it's good enough to go to jail in. You knew we were coming. You shoulda been dressed and had your hair combed by the time we got here. I hate it when people aren't ready!"

"I hate you! I bet you're not married cause no woman can stand you jerk!"

"You're right. I'm not married but it's by choice. I'm waiting for Mrs. Right. I don't want to end up marrying a gun toting, drive-by shooting, knife stabbing woman such as yourself," McIntosh laughed.

"It's not funny!" the woman sobbed. "I did everything to please that man and he still didn't want me. Why couldn't he love me like I loved him? When I couldn't get him to love me, I turned to the opposite of love, anger. Screw him! Screw everybody! I'm tired of being nice to people!" she concluded.

WAKE UP!

sister teacher
ask me to give up my pain
want me to jus' leave it
like they always leave me
like my daddy leave me

sister teacher say fly
it's time... she say
don't know my pain

stare at me through my mornin' coffee
my pain is my lunch time lover
my pain colds my sheets 'fore I get in bed at
night

sister teacher don't know

I be afraid
If I don't feel pain
I ain't gonna feel at all.

Rhonda L. Mithcell

"It doesn't pay to be nice! From now on, Camille is going to take charge of her life and relationships by doing whatever I want. No more compromising! I'm gonna see whomever I want, whenever I want. The only thing that matters is me!"

The new and improved Camille wasn't going to waste her time with anyone whom she felt didn't deserve to be with her. Naturally, a change in wardrobe and hair style automatically came with her change in attitude. Within a month, all her credit cards became maxed out from long and unnecessary shopping sprees. To this day, Camille's closet is still cluttered with dresses and shoes she bought during this period of her life. She bought all kinds of dresses. Some casual, short, formal, semi-short, low cut, long with a high slit and extra short with a low cut. Some of the dresses were never removed from their plastic wrapping. Many of the shoes she bought were never taken out of their boxes.

One day while at the hair salon, Camille's extremely handsome and flamboyant gay hairdresser asked her to represent his salon in a hair show given at a local hotel. Camille agreed.

"Camille, girl you gotta be in my show honey! I can really show my stuff with your hair girl! You gotta do it, do it!" he sweetly pleaded.

"Okay, I'll do it. It should be fun."

"Great! I've got an idea! Can I change your hair color?"

"Sure. What are you going to change it to?"

"I'mma change it to an N6 girl!"

"What' a N6?" Camille asked.

"That's just beautician stuff. All our hair colors are numbered. Don't worry. You'll look fine girl!"

To be different, he took her black hair and dyed to something called an N6 that turned out to be a bright auburn/orange color. According to him, the color accentuated her caramel skin color and brown eyes. As Camille stood in the mirror accessing the damage and listening to his sales pitch, she thought, "With a little Tomango lip stick made by Mack and I'll be looking good!"

After the show, numerous people approached Camille and complimented her on her hair color. Camille was sold. Her hair was looking good and no one else could tell her it didn't, although her brother did but she never listened to him anyway.

"Who cared what anyone else thought anyway, especially men!" she thought.

Camille's naturally big warm heart was growing cold and bitter toward men. She didn't want any part of one unless she could benefit the most from the relationship. Of course, this was what she was constantly trying to convince herself. In reality, this wasn't the true Camille. The true Camille was very helpful, loving and giving to almost everyone, especially her man. The facade she was now showing to men was only there to disguise her vulnerability. She wanted to shield herself from the pain of being mistreated again. In the long run, Camille's new character hurt her. She forced some nice men out of her life when she really wanted them around.

The first victim to be stricken out of Camille's life uncharacteristically by her new attitude was a guy by the name of Patrick. Patrick and Camille casually became acquainted while at school one day. He was sort of a friend of a friend who knew one of her friends. Fortunately, this gave Camille the opportunity to do a thorough background check on this brother before she started to date him. It was revealed to her that Patrick was a well mannered, athletic guy who always dressed well. Like her, Patrick was also a struggling college student who still lived at home with his parents.

Even though Camille was able to use her contacts and find out that he was harmless, she still proceeded to date him with extreme caution. She'd had one too many men turn from Dr. Love into Mr. Hyde. Camille was determined not to let it happen again. In her defense, she developed a cold, hard and somewhat rude personality. If Camille wanted to see Patrick, she would. If not, she wouldn't, no matter how much he persisted. His needs were not what mattered. Too many times, Camille had sacrificed her time and submitted to her partner's demands but not any damn more!

Patrick could have been considered a good catch but there were a few minor things about him and his situation Camille found disturbing. The first thing she found disturbing was that Patrick had a poor relationship with his mother. In one aspect, Camille could see why. Patrick's Mom didn't appear to be a very caring person toward her children nor did she appear to be positive or driven to achieve any higher goals. In Camille's opinion, she just seemed to be around occupying space. Sometimes she worked part-time but mostly she stayed at home doing nothing.

Another thing that bothered her was that no one in the family owned a car, including Patrick. In fact, once he had the audacity to call Camille's mother on the phone when Camille wasn't home. Patrick then asked Camille's mother to drop him off at school. Being the generous person she was, she phoned her job and told them she would be late. Camille's mother then drove Patrick to school.

Soon, Camille and her family looked at Patrick as a codependent that they were unable to claim on taxes. Camille fed him and clothed him. At one time or another, everyone in her family gave him some sort of brotherly advice which was impossible to get at his home. Eventually, she had no choice but to drop him like a hot potato! After all, it was all about Camille now. Any other time Camille probably would have taken Patrick in like a wounded animal and nurtured him back to health. Not this time. Her primary objective was to achieve self-gratification, nothing more.

The next big strike was Christopher. Christopher was six years Camille's senior. He was an entertainment promoter who juggled his time between the music studios and out of town events. Being the very kind and considerate person he was, Christopher would thoughtfully phone Camille from whatever city he was visiting. They would then commence to converse for hours. Disappointingly, their short relationship mainly consisted of long distance phone calls and quick lunches between business appointments.

Without a doubt, most women would have considered him a good catch. For Camille, there was one important element of his life she questioned.

"Where exactly would I fit in?" Christopher had no time for her. She needed someone who could give her lots of love and attention. Camille enjoyed hugging as well as being hugged back. She needed someone who would be there physically as well as spiritually. Christopher's job didn't allow him to meet her needs on that level. Camille felt frustrated. She knew what she wanted was at her fingertips but yet so far out of reach. Camille had no choice but to give Christopher his release papers. Remember, now it was all about Camille and what she wanted!

The third strike belonged to a gentleman by the name of Timothy. Timothy was a well built, stern and domineering police officer whom she met early one morning while buying coffee at a convenience store. Camille couldn't forget! As she pulled into the parking lot, she was met by the stares of about six doughnut eating and coffee guzzling police officers. They were standing around their patrol cars talking and eating as if there were no crime in the city. As she stepped out of the car and warded off the stares, one officer in particular caught her attention. For some strange reason, this one seemed to stand out from the rest.

Trying not to make it too obvious, Camille nonchalantly glanced back at the officer and gave him the "Go ahead" smile before she proceeded to confidently walk into the store. Her woman's intuition told her that sooner or later, he'd follow. Camille poured herself a cup of coffee and glanced back to see if she had company but she had no such luck. From that point, she bought herself some more time by browsing around in the candy/gum section.

"Hi! How are you this morning?" a stern voice asked from behind. "My name is Tim."

Turning around, she saw the officer standing there armed with a huge smile on his face. Matching his smile and extending her hand for a shake, she answered, "Hi Tim. I'm Camille and I'm doing fine thanks."

"You look nice this morning," he followed.

"Thank you. So do you."

Tim looked directly into her eyes and with authority asked, "Can I have your phone number?"

The officer's directness totally caught Camille off guard. He completely violated the player's code of ethics by skipping over the small talk and getting directly to the point. She didn't even get a chance to asses his physical qualities as well as his mental stability. For all she knew, he could have been a fat doughnut eating serial killer or something. The forcefulness of his voice intimidated Camille and made her feel as though she didn't have a choice in the matter.

"Can I tell a police officer in uniform no?" she asked herself. Camille didn't really want to flat-out tell him no, especially since she had lead him to her. So instead, Camille panicked and gave him her mother's phone number.

"Thanks! I'll give you a call later. Nice meeting you!" he concluded as he walked away.

Tim gave her the impression he only wanted her phone number for statistical purposes. It was probably a game he played all day. Camille didn't think he had any intentions of calling her.

"Camille! Camille!" her mother shouted across the house. "You've got a phone call on my phone!"

When she heard what her mother was shouting, Tim didn't immediately come to mind because a few of her old school mates still called her on that number. Besides, it had been three days since she had met him. Camille had almost forgotten about him.

After picking up the phone and finding out it was Tim on the other end, Camille became surprised and intrigued to hear what he had to say. He appeared intelligent and had a soothing personality. So much, she apprehensively accepted his invitation to visit him at his residence that was something Camille rarely did.

Tim impressively lived in a house located in a nice middle-class neighborhood, all alone, no wife and no children. In talking to him, Camille quickly discovered he had his whole life planned out. He had everything figured out from when he wanted to get married, where he wanted to live, what type of person he was looking for and what she had to posses. He also made it damn clear that he wasn't looking for a wife or a girlfriend at the moment. "So what does he want from me then?"

Camille's guess was it was for sex only.

Mr. Officer made what she called, a feeble attempt to spend some quality time with her. First, he requested that she accompany him to the mall and help him purchase a painting for his home. Camille out-right refused to go.

"Why would I want to go to the mall with him and he wasn't going to buy me anything?"

Second, Tim asked Camille to go out for pizza.

"Oh pizza huh? I'm sorry but I've made other plans," she told him when she didn't have plans.

"Why would I want to go eat pizza with Tim when I know he doesn't want a girlfriend and probably not me for company. There are at least six men listed in my phone book whom if I requested, would gladly treat me to a sea food dinner and not expect anything in return from me."

The more Camille spoke to Tim, the more intimidated she became. She formulated the opinion that if she were going to get with him, she'd have to get her act together. As it was, she was only a senior in college with a part-time job as a bank teller. Tim was settled while her future was up for grabs. With the grace of God, she could turn out to be a Ph.D. or a college grad flipping burgers. Even though she enjoyed his company, Camille made a conscious effort to avoid seeing him again. Although their relationship didn't blossom into a full-blown love affair, they still managed to remain in close contact with one another by becoming close telephone mates.

As time progressed, she couldn't tell that Tim needed her friendship so he could stay in touch with the civilian world. He hated being around cops all the time, on duty and off. Camille became his mediator between the cop world and civilian life. Often, he would use her patient and understanding ear as a wastebasket for his job frustrations. On a few occasions, his job related problems hit Camille where it hurt, in her past.

"How was work today?" she would ask Tim as if he had something new to say.

"It was horrible! How else could it be? Last night I responded to this domestic violence call where this woman got her butt kicked by her boyfriend. That was the second time I'd taken a report from woman this year. It doesn't make any sense. Why do these women keep going back for more abuse?"

Camille really didn't have an exact answer to his question. For every woman the reason was different. For her, it may have been love, attention or insecurity. She didn't really know why but for whatever the reason was, she kept going back for more also.

"I don't know Tim. Maybe the lady couldn't financially afford to leave her boyfriend," she suggested.

"No that couldn't be it cause neither of them had a job. Her welfare check is probably supporting both of them and their kids. She'd probably be better off financially without him. I just don't get it. Why would a woman stay with a man who abuses her and not want him to go to jail?" he asked with frustration. "That's so damn stupid!"

"Maybe she can't find anyone else or maybe it's because. . ."

Cutting Camille off in the middle of her sentence, he asked, "Why are women always making excuses for each other as if they understand one another? You don't know how that lady feels Camille. You've never been through what she has been through so how can you make excuses for her?"

"I'm not making excuses for her, I'm just trying to supply some possible answers that's all."

"I don't think anyone can. Let me ask you this, would you ever let a man hit you and then go back to him?"

Although she immediately knew the answer to this one, Camille had to pause and give some serious thought as to whether or not she was going to answer it truthfully. She didn't know Tim all that well. She figured that if she answered truthfully by saying, "Yes I would go back to him and it has happened to me," he would have probably thought less of her. Camille's troubled past was not really a secret because she had confessed it to some of her friends on other occasions when the topic came up, not in detail of course.

"Nope! I'd never let anyone hit me and then go back to him," she falsely answered out loud. In her mind, she concluded her answer with, "At least not anymore I wouldn't."

Camille and Tim always had something to talk about. Unfortunately, everything they talked about wasn't always on a positive note. He was always so direct, confident and almost emotionless seventy-five percent of the time they talked. Sometimes his comments would be downright rude, even the ones directed at her.

"Why did you dye your hair burgundy? Do you think that's cute? I mean, what's the story behind it?" Tim asked Camille on more than one occasion.

"Shut up! You're so negative. You remind me of someone else I use to know!"

"I'm not trying to hurt your feelings. I'm just trying to get an understanding as to why your hair looks like it's on fire or something."

On the positive side, Tim's ever-flowing sarcasm and rudeness produced some good ideas. All he needed to do was exercise some tact and he would have been fine. Tim was a perfectionist that made him almost impossible to deal with. He expected the same from everyone he became involved with. It didn't matter if his friends were male, female or casual acquaintance. He had high expectations from them all.

What immediately caught Camille's attention was how easily he was able to ward off her verbal attacks. Camille was under the impression that his feelings were shielded and unaffected by life's obstacles. His feelings and emotions seemed unreachable. Timothy's appeared to have armor plated emotions. He gave Camille the impression he didn't give a darn about anybody or anything. This was something she desperately wanted to do but couldn't.

In a weird sense, Tim became somewhat of a mentor to Camille. Tim in his own distorted way also offered a lot of positive words of encouragement when no one else did. Camille didn't like the fact he'd sometimes joke and say, "Your hair is jacked-up," and "You're ghetto. Tim swore he was only joking but she wasn't so sure.

"You know what Camille?" he'd say. "I can tell you're a very smart and intelligent woman. I know you're going to be very successful someday in the near future that is if somebody is willing to hire you with burgundy hair. Who knows, maybe you can be a psychologist for the circus?"

Tim was a good listener but not always good at empathizing. He wasn't a very good problem solver either. His answer to everything was always, "Screw it! Who cares, do whatever you want to do and then let someone else worry about it!" That was always a goal of Camille's but rarely an actual act. Internally, she adored Tim for the strength and extreme confidence he had in himself. Unfortunately, for those reasons, she felt sad they could never become closer because she felt intimidated. Camille did her best to push him away.

Camille created a series of harsh and rude test to distinguish the men from the boys. If she spotted a weakness in a man's personality, she would viciously attack it. She figured that she'd get them before they got her. Causing someone to get upset gave Camille the immediate short-term satisfaction of being strong and tough. Very few men were able to withstand the abuse. Many of those who stayed around were old friends from high school who knew her before the heartaches distorted her thinking. Camille described her actions as a test. In reality, she was only testing herself to see how fast she could get rid of people.

In time, Camille suffered the same psychological symptoms as abused children have when they grow up and became parents. Somehow, her role had suddenly shifted from being the abused to becoming the abuser. Camille's verbal attacks were so vicious that she should have worn a "Beware of dog!" sign around her neck. Anyone who tried to get too close or who told her they cared, got dogged. Camille was fed up with people who said they cared and then hurt her. Like an abusing parent, she set unrealistic goals for friends both male and female. When they would fail to meet her expectations, she became extremely stressed out. The verbal abuse then followed. Camille thought everyone viewed her as messed up because that's how she viewed herself.

"Camille darling! Why are you doing this to yourself?" her mother asked.

Snarling with confusion, Camille asked, "Why am I doing what?"

Camille's mother was not only displaying her normal look of concern, she also had an expression of internal pain. "Why are you constantly getting yourself involved in these unhealthy relationships?"

Now frowning with anger, Camille couldn't believe she would ask such a stupid question. The answer was simple!

"I don't intentionally get involved in bad relationships. They just happen and then they're hard to get out of, that's all!" Camille snapped.

Mom now appeared more hurt. She realized Camille didn't really understand why she was doing what she was doing. The pain was visibly exhibited in mom's voice.

"I know what you're doing honey. You can't live my life! The relationship that your father and me have is not normal. You can't live like I have. I'm content with my situation. It's not bothering me because I've learned to deal with it. You don't have to deal with it honey cause you have a choice."

Her question suddenly took on a different meaning to Camille. "Maybe that wasn't such a stupid question after all? Hum. . . am I feeling useless because of my father's neglect or because I watched my mother endure the absence of love from her mate? Am I subconsciously following the plight of my mother's misery as she had said? Perhaps I am attracted to men who are extremely nice and attentive to my needs because I view those acts as compensation for what my mother missed?" Camille wondered.

Acts of attention and gifts of monetary value were very important to Camille. As a child monetary gifts played a significant role in her life. Whenever Camille's parents told her they loved her, they'd follow the statement up with a gift. In time, one came synonymous with the other. That's why an expensive dinner, flowers and other things of material value became so important to her. If Camille weren't offered those things then she would assume the person didn't care.

Take Timothy for an example, communication was his basic need but she couldn't see that initially. All Timothy really needed was Camille's companionship and ear. There was no way she could see that. Camille had never before experienced that with someone on Timothy's level. He was single, owned his own home and had a good job. The most disturbing part was his independence. He didn't need Camille! At least not in the sense she had defined the word need. She hastily concluded Timothy didn't care for her. Why? Because he didn't offer something monetary like all those before him and after her parents.

Camille would have felt better if Timothy, Patrick and Mark would have still lived at home with their parents, been unemployed, uneducated and needed someone to help them get ahead. Then she could have filled out job applications for them and assumed a role she understood. Camille probably would have felt more secure in the relationships. She needed to work in her relationships. She had to feel as though she could help her man grow and improve himself. In that way, she could feel valuable and special. The most flattering and uplifting thing she ever heard a man say was not, "I love you!" or "I care about you!" It was, "If it wasn't for you, I wouldn't be where I am now!" Unfortunately she ignored her own needs and incurable problems.

Another thing Timothy, Patrick and Mark had in common was that they were all looking for a deep friendship first before falling in love. For Camille, loving a friend was too much to ask. Friends communicated, disclose themselves and understood one another. She couldn't handle that.

Camille's insides were dark, depressing, distorted and ugly. She didn't feel good about herself. She constantly hurt from loneliness. Her loneliness wasn't from an absence of company. It was from not being understood. No one knew what she had gone through nor did anyone understand what she was currently feeling.

On the outside, Camille was all smiles. She demonstrated strength and confidence. Her noticeable leadership qualities got her elected president of her sorority chapter. As president of her sorority, she successfully coordinated community events, fund-raisers and various functions. Certainly, not the type of task a weak, insecure and lonely person could handle. On the contrary, it happened.

Statistically, Camille possessed and uncanny number of friends and associates from sorority and school. Even still, she felt alone and especially misunderstood. Her constant inner turmoil frequently took her on emotional roller coaster rides. Everything could go along fine and then someone could unintentionally say something to piss her off. Out of nowhere she'd explode.

At this unstable junction in her life, Camille was so insecure that she couldn't openly accept any criticism what so ever. Throughout her life, men had demonstrated to Camille that she wasn't good enough to be in their company. Her father who wrongfully abandoned her spiritually first showed it. Then, Camille was lead to believe she caused problems for all the others. For Kelvin she did it by not surrendering her virginity. In James' case, she wasn't submissive enough. With Tyrell she was too aggressive. Finally, with Mark she was too aloof with the relationship.

In every case, it was naturally assumed she was at fault. If something went wrong, just blame Camille and she'd accept the responsibility! And of course she did. Taking the blame hurt Camille. Unfortunately, emotional hurt and anguish were something she was accustomed to. She started feeling it early in her life. Even though her mother denied suffering, Camille could still feel her mom's emotional distress and emptiness.

"Is this also my destiny? Am I going to marry someone who cheats on me and then abandons me emotionally?"

Camille's parent's emotional separation was so that severe they couldn't even bare to do something as simple as sit down on the couch and watch television together. Eating breakfast together at the kitchen table was out of the question. Witnessing her parent's separation caused Camille excruciating pain.

Personal experience also caused feelings of being unwanted and alienation. Tyrell showed gratitude by sitting at the far end of the couch with his feet extended in Camille's direction. It was as if he were defending his space. To make it worse, he also tried to ignore her presence by starring at the t.v. like she wasn't there. Dialogue, warmth and affection were definitely absent. Like her mother, Camille stayed in the relationship.

"Perhaps unhappiness is my fate after all?"

STRIKE FOUR!

Some people say time can heal all wounds. That wasn't true in Camille's case. Two years should have been plenty of time for Camille to get over the ill effects of her past relationship with Tyrell. Unfortunately, there were still a few open sores left in her mind from the relationship. People also say breakups only occur when two people stop loving each other. Camille wasn't exactly sure if it was true in their case. All she knew was that she gave the relationship her all and it still failed. That's why she gave it up.

Camille was frustrated. It had been over two years since she last dated Tyrell. For some reason, she still had a need to confront the abuser personally. She needed to understand why it happened. She also had to prove to herself that she was a strong person. Camille wasn't exactly sure why she still felt this way after all this time. Perhaps it was because Tyrell had never been completely eliminated from her life. Even though she knew she no longer loved him and pretty sure he didn't love her either, they continued to accept one another as friends.

In the two years she hadn't been involved with Tyrel, he graduated from college. Tyrell progressed from an angry struggling athlete whose career was over, to an extremely caring and bourgeois district aid to a California congressman. Tyrell's attire had transitioned from musty sweat suits to expensive suits and cologne. Confident, reassuring and positive, he was hardly the person she once knew. As a representative to a congressman, he was given the opportunity to rub elbows with a lot of important people.

Every now and then, Tyrell would pop over to Camille's house while visiting friends and family in the area. Other times, he'd call just to say hello and see how she was doing. It didn't seem possible but Tyrell appeared to be suffering some ill effects of his own from the way he treated her. Perhaps guilt was eating away at his consciousness. Sometimes he'd call and ask Camille to escort him to job related functions. He did this even though she once told him she would never go out with him again. Every now and then, he would ask Camille if she needed anything to eat and then offer to bring it to her. According to him, he also did a lot of career net working on her behalf since he sat on a couple of college boards.

Camille's life seemed to be pretty much on track, except for that one psychological wall which still stood in her way. No matter what she did, the effects of the relationship still lingered about. Although she didn't have problems talking about the abuse. She was still in a state of denial about how the relationship affected her current situations. She couldn't admit to anyone, including herself that her current attitude was a direct result of her traumatic relationship with Tyrell.

Camille desperately needed to face Tyrell on more of a personal level. She had to show herself that the problems he caused were over. Besides, he was being so overly nice and generous she felt she deserved what he was offering. If giving was his way of trying to right the wrong he did then receiving was her way of correcting the mistakes she allowed to happen.

"So what are you doing tonight?" Tyrell asked.

"I don't know. I'm hungry so I might go get myself something to eat."

"I can take you to get something if you want."

Breaking her three-year vow, Camille nonchalantly answered, "Okay, where do you feel like going?"

A look of shock and disbelief appeared on his face as he dropped his mouth wide open and asked,

"For real?" A smirk remained on his face as if he were waiting for me to deliver a punch line to a joke. "No not for real silly!"

Camille's acceptance was certainly no joke. In her mind, the first step of the healing process had begun. With dinner, soon came a movie, more dinners, lunch and late night snacks. Camille experienced a strange felling while being around the new Tyrell. It wasn't DeJa Vu' as she thought it would be. It was almost as if she were with a totally different person all together. It was almost as if his body had been cloned. Tyrell's mind and thoughts were of a kinder and more gentle person.

Next came the sex! Camille didn't know where that part was supposed to fit into the scheme of things but it somehow became a big part of the game. About this time, she was casually going out with a couple of guys. Since there was no way she could be intimate with more than one person at a time, Tyrell became it. The sad part about that was she really couldn't see herself in a committed relationship with him.

The sex was his while the rest of her dated whomever. Some of the men she dated had the potential to become boyfriends. Unfortunately, there wasn't any hope of Camille finding out if her assumptions were accurate. The separation of her mind and body prohibited her from being able to take a relationship with another man to a higher level. Camille couldn't visualize herself married to Tyrell but she figured that since he never left her life, they'd probably end up married.

RING! RING!

"Oh good! Must be Tyrell calling to ask me if I need anything," she thought. Acting on her assumptions, Camille picked up the phone and yelled, "Hi Honey!"

"Sorry! It's not honey. Do you want me to let you go so you call honey?" Timothy asked.

A little disappointed, Camille answered without first thinking. "No that's alright. How's life and work?" "Oops! Why did I ask him about work?" she thought.

"Life is fine, work sucks! Last night I arrested this woman for stabbing her boyfriend in the chest. How refreshing it was!"

"She probably did it because he hit her," Camille responded.

"Oh, he did hit her. In fact, he hit her all the time but not last night when he got stabbed. This time, all he did was yell at her and piss her off. That's how women are. They like to hold in things until they explode. They get violent over something as simple as an argument."

"Well, sometimes it's hard to vent out your frustrations when you really want something to work."

With each second, Camille could feel Timothy's blood pressure bubbling like brewing coffee. He just didn't understand. The more she tried to make him, the more frustrated he got. Actually, neither one of them was really trying to understand each other. Timothy was trying to tell Camille not to have a victim's mentality and she was trying to tell Timothy she already had one.

"If your man hits you once, there is a good chance he'll do it again and again. I see it every day. Every call I go to, I always ask the woman if it's the first time her man hit her. Nine out of ten times the woman says he's done it before. What I can't understand is why in the hell do women always try to make an abusive relationship work? They need to just get the hell out?" Timothy shouted.

Now, Camille's blood pressure was boiling. "Why are you so negative toward women? That's why no one ever wants to call the police!"

"If you women would open up your eyes you wouldn't need the police. I could arrest a woman for domestic violence every night and not feel a thing!"

"You know what Timothy?" Camille shouted in anger before catching herself and regaining composure. "Never mind. Screw it! I don't want to talk about this with you anymore."

"That's because you know I'm right. I'm always right, huh, Camille?" he rubbed it in.

Even though Tyrell had indeed changed, ever so often Camille would look at him and see him as he was, "Tyrell the Tyrant!" Her intuitive mother was not impressed by his resurrection. She thought that he went out of his way to persuade himself and others that he was a different person. Immediately upon coming in contact with Camille's mother, Tyrell would extend his hand for a handshake and then assume a professional tone of voice.

"Good evening Mrs. Sanders. How are you doing ma'am?"

Camille would think to herself, "What a joke! Who does he think he is? Camille's mother had known Tyrell since he was a child looking for a ride home after dark.

"Knock if off Tyrell! We knew you when you didn't have a job!" Camille would say.

Changing topics, Camille mentioned that she was dating Tyrell again. Timothy didn't know of the violence that took place between them years ago. All he knew was she dumped him because he was inconsiderate, mean and sometimes verbally abusive. Camille put it casually, "He said mean things to me."

For some reason, Camille candidly began explaining her rationale for believing Tyrell would someday be her husband even though she wasn't in love with him.

"I wonder what Timothy has to say about it?" she thought.

"That's stupid Camille! How can you end up marrying someone just because they're always in your life? Transients are always in your life too. Why don't you marry one? Roaches never leave either," Timothy responded.

"I wonder if he'd buy me a big wedding ring?" Camille pondered out loud.

"He'll probably buy you a big ring, a big house, a big car and then take it all back when you guys get a big divorce because you're not happy. Nobody changes that much!"

Four months of eating, talking and routinely having sex had gone by when Camille shockingly discovered her period hadn't come. That had never happened before. Camille's body clock always ran exactly on time as if it were a finely built Swiss watch. She became terrified when she realized something was wrong. Her mind and thoughts ran rapid.

"Oh no! I'm pregnant," she thought. "I'm going to have to leave the masters program at school and be a full time mama."

The most frightening part of it was that Tyrell being the father. She wondered how he would react? Her past experiences with him revealed that he didn't respond well to stress. Tyrell was a friend, someone to talk to, date and have sex with but not someone to have a baby with. Camille didn't love him anymore nor could she ever again.

"If I don't love him then why am I sleeping with him?"

That night when Tyrell came over to visit, the atmosphere was tense. He knew something was wrong the moment he walked through the door. The tears in Camille's eyes were slight clues.

"What's wrong?" he immediately asked.

"I have something to tell you Tyrell."

"What?"

"My period didn't come."

"Do you think you're pregnant?"

"I've never missed one before."

Sighing and rubbing the sweat from his forehead, he asked, "What are you going to do?"

"I don't know. What do you want me to do?" Camille asked.

Tyrell then went on to say that he would be supportive to the end regardless of whatever decision she made. He then sincerely apologized for not being a bigger man and for not being more responsible. From there, he went into the basic bullshit line most men say to their pregnant girlfriends.

"Whatever you do, I'm here for you honey. I don't want you to go through this alone."

The next morning, Camille went to her local drug store and bought a home pregnancy test. She carefully read the instructions at least three times before finally getting enough nerve to give it a try. She was so nervous that she couldn't urinate. Then when she did, her hands trembled so much that urine ran through her fingers. Making a last second prayer, she checked the indicator and the results read negative! Another test by her doctor concluded she was not pregnant. Now she felt blessed. Not because she wasn't pregnant but because she had been shown a sign. The sign read, "Tyrell is not good for you. He is taking up valuable space."

That night, Camille phoned Tyrell and gave him the test results. She also gave him the end result of the lesson she'd learned.

"I'm sorry Tyrell. I can no longer see you in the way I was. I can't continue having sex with you when I know I don't see a positive future in it. We can still be friends if you want but not on that level ever again."

Tyrell didn't verbally object. He graciously accepted her decree which lowered his status from lover to a casual buddy. He still phoned every now and then to see how she was doing. Also, which Camille wasn't sure why, he desperately insisted she let him have his car insurance mail come to her address. His excuse was the area where he lived was redlined which caused his insurance premium to be twice higher than if he used his address.

"Your sister lives just around the corner Tyrell. Why can't you have your mail go to her house?" Camille once asked him.

"Aw Camille. Me and her don't get along too well. She may not tell me it's there and cause me to get dropped from my policy," he rebutted.

One thought crossed her mind. Perhaps the real reason he wanted to have his mail come to her address was so he could have a reason to come over, try to talk his way into having sex and then screw his way back into a steady relationship with her. It worked once but she seriously doubted she could let it ever happen again. She couldn't see him in that way anymore. Also, him coming over to pick up his mail gave Tyrell an excuse to stop by and check on her life.

Camille agreed to let him have his mail come to her address. Tyrell was finally behind her. The chapter on Tyrell was finally closed.

BEHIND THE SMILES AND LAUGHTER

1 is a prime number and can be used when describing a single solitary action.

1 is the number of orgasms I had during our 2 1/2 year marriage.

1 is the number of times you asked if I were faking it, I wish the Academy
knew about those performances.

1 time you slept with my best friend, then asked could I possibly forgive you.

1 loud and long "Hell no you're crazy" shot from my lips. Call me a sapphire.

1 ass kickin' followed. Yours. You dialed 9-11

1 time I called the police. Lights, Sirens, Action. Now you know that 357. was only
for show. I still had one more bitch to deal with.

1 more chance you begged... and all that got you was 1 stiletto heel planted
squarely in your chest, and a view of heaven as I walked directly over you and out the door.

1 bitter bitch? No, just 1 lesson thoroughly learned.

Rhonda L. Mitchell

Camille and a couple of her girlfriends started hitting the club scene pretty hard. Practically, every other night, they partied their asses off at a nightclub somewhere in the city. Guys would come out of the woodworks and buy Camille and her girlfriends drinks hoping one of them would give up a phone number or more.

On one particular night, a well-dressed gentleman in a suit and tie smoothly approached Camille. The tall man debonairly held a drink in one hand. Ted is who he introduced himself as. His smooth, clean, face sported a handsome smile. He gave Camille the impression he was a nice person. Her initial pre-phone number screening told Camille he had a steady job as an electrician. From their conversation, Ted gave her a good and satisfying feeling. She felt it was okay to talk via the telephone. Before leaving the club, she and Ted and exchanged phone numbers.

Reaching down, Camille gently held up Ted's left hand to eye level. She curiously examined his ring finger for a wedding band. When one was absent, she then carefully checked around the finger to see if he had any discoloration on the finger from an emergency ring removal.

"How come a nice guy like you is not married? Or are you?" Camille flirtatiously asked.

"Nope. I'm not married, you don't see any rings on my finger do you?"

With a smile, she stated, "That doesn't mean a thing! Have you ever been married?"

With a straight face he answered, "Nope! Never."

"Do you have any children?"

"Yep. I have a daughter."

Camille smiled and then tried to sound happy and excited. She acted as if she thought he was lucky or special for having a child out of wedlock. "Oh, how nice! I bet you're a good father!"

The final result revealed Ted as kind and thoughtful. He appeared to be tailor made for Camille. So, why did he have to have a child? The man was right but not his family situation.

Camille hated men with children! Children were nothing more than a life size reminder that someone else had screwed the father first. Also, the whole parental situation often created big headaches for everyone involved with either the mother or the Daddy. Usually, parents dedicate the remainder of their lives to making the other unhappy. They constantly call each other to bitch about money, kids and child custody. Camille was too young to deal with that bull! She wasn't ready to play mommy to anybody's child!

One thing eventually led to another. Ted turned out to be a really nice, fun loving person who enjoyed going out and doing fun things. His outgoing personality along with his desire to go on fun dates like Disneyland, Magic Mountain and Sea World, lured Camille into his web like a spider capturing a fly. Camille considered it a plus when Ted took her on dates to amusements parks at the beginning of their relationship. To her, a date at an amusement park told her a lot about Ted. Unlike the normal confining hour-long dinner date, she utilized the many hours they spent standing in line waiting to board rides on assessing her partner. She found out that her date was a good conversationalist and patient. Most all, he was fun and easygoing. In her opinion, it would have been pretty hard for Ted to maintain a front in his personality for that extended time and around so many people. Camille was having a great time with Ted and it showed. She constantly smiled from ear to ear.

For the moment she was safe. Ted's personality, energy and charisma were overwhelming. Camille had no choice but to hang in there for a while.

She decided to stick around until she gathered enough information about his parenting situation. Then she would make a fair decision.

As she had figured, the more time she spent with Ted, the more she saw him take on the symptoms of a separated father. Sometimes she could tell he was carrying some heavy issues on his mind. Ted's attention would often drift. For no apparent reason, he'd suddenly stare aimlessly into space or at a wall.

Camille was concerned. She often thought his sudden immobility and mind detachment was caused by something she had said or did.

"What's wrong honey? Are you okay?"

Leaping back into the present, he'd answer, "Oh! I'm fine. I was just thinking about something, that's all."

"What were you thinking about?"

"Nothing much really. Just some things that I need to attend to."

Camille naturally assumed Ted was going through some problems regarding his child and the baby's mama.

"Whatever the reason is, it has to be something of a serious nature to take over his thoughts while he is kicking it with me! Maybe I reminded him of his baby's mama or maybe something I said triggered a flashback?" Camille thought.

Regardless, something was definitely wrong! Using her past situations as a reference source, Camille didn't want to aggravate the problem by seemingly prying into his personal life. She refused to ask Ted questions about what he was thinking. She was confident eventually, when he was ready, he would share his deep personal feelings with her.

It was only about three months into the relationship when for some unknown reason, Ted decided it was the right time to finally break down and tell Camille what was going on inside his head. Several weeks prior, his uneasiness alerted her this day of admonition was drawing nearer.

"I need to talk to you honey," Ted solemnly told Camille.

"What about?"

Of course, Camille had a pretty good idea what was going to be about. Her mind was prepared to hear him tell her it was over. He was going back to his baby's mamma. Her only hope was the sentence would be handed down swiftly. It wasn't. Unfortunately, Ted dragged his point out to the fullest. It was as if he were following the outline to a "Star

Wars" movie which started off with, "A long, long time ago. . ."

Looking Camille sincerely in the eye, he started. "When I was seventeen years old, I dated this girl. . ." From there he went to, "When I was nineteen, I got this same girl pregnant. . ." Then to, when I reached twenty, we got married. . ."

A red flag went off in Camille's head. "Wait just a damn minute! When I first met him, he told me he had never been married before!" she thought to herself.

Camille made a strong effort to be calm. She was at least going to wait until he got finished with the part about his divorce before she went off. Ted never got to that part. Instead, the news got worse.

"My wife and I have been separated on four different occasions. This time it's been almost five months since we've been together and I have no intentions of going back to her again. I just wish she wasn't pregnant."

"Pregnant? Did he say pregnant?"

Now seemed like the perfect time for Camille to blow her stack. "Why in the hell did you lie to me Ted?" she tearfully yelled. "I trusted you and then you lied! Why does everybody do that?"

"I'm sorry Camille. I wanted to tell you sooner but I knew you wouldn't get involved with me if you knew about my situation."

"You damn right I wouldn't! In fact, I'm not gonna deal with this crap now! Good bye!"

A couple of seconds later, Camille walked out the door feeling hurt, betrayed and wanting to rid herself of Ted forever. On the way home, she weighed the pros and cons of being involved with a separated man who has one and a half children. What bothered her most was he out-right lied about being married.

"What else did he lie about? Maybe he has six kids?"

On the positive side, at least he did eventually tell her the truth. There was a good chance she probably wouldn't have found out on her own. She had already snooped and dug through his apartment. In her investigation, she came up with no evidence of another woman whatsoever.

"Everyone makes mistakes. Would it be right for me to abandon him after he had been so near perfect? His only mistake was made years ago."

Camille was pretty sure if the situation had been reversed, Ted would have probably tried to hang in for her. By the time she had arrived home, Camille had talked herself into feeling sorry for a man who had just admitted he lied and betrayed her trust. Good ole Camille, once again talked herself back into a relationship that deep down inside, she didn't want. Later on that day, Ted called and humbly apologized for being deceitful and Camille accepted his apology with an open heart.

Camille made it a point not to express her unhappiness to Ted a second time. However, she did manage to accidentally mention her dissatisfaction with Ted in a phone conversation with "Officer Insensitivity", Timothy. Normally, domestic violence and relationships were two topics she usually tried to veer from when speaking with Timothy. It was obvious Timothy had a negative attitude toward women. Unfortunately, Camille was in dire need of a reality check. She needed someone to point her in the right direction or to give her moral support. Ted couldn't balance his own troubled life so it was useless for him to try and assist Camille in stabilizing her's. She turned to Timothy.

"Hi Camille. How's everything going? What have you been doing?"

"Everything is fine. I've just been going out, that's all."

"Anybody interesting? Maybe a love connection?" he asked.

"It could have been but this guy has problems."

Not really taking the time to think about the consequences of explaining her situation to Mr. Negativity, she then painfully told Timothy about her involvement with Ted and his family situation. At the conclusion of her tale, Camille knew whatever came out of Timothy's mouth was going to be negative and piss her off.

"If you don't wanna be with this guy then why are you wasting both of you guys time by dating?" Timothy asked.

"I don't look at it as me wasting my time. He takes me to a lot of fun places. I enjoy his company."

The inflection in Timothy's voice changed as he said, "You see. . . That's why I never take women anywhere! If a man is decent looking, nice, courteous and willing to cough up some bucks for an expensive dinner, most women will automatically continue to date this guy even when they don't care for him. They do it just to be doing something. Screw that!"

"It's not like that. I really like this guy."

"I'm sure you do. And I'm sure one day you'll enjoy babysitting his children and taking money out of your check to support his wife and kids," he sarcastically stated.

"Timothy, shut the hell up! I don't want to hear that!" Camille angrily shouted.

"Yes you do! You know how I feel about relationships! You wanted to hear me say it cause you can't admit it to yourself! You know I'm right. I'm always right."

Timothy may have had a valid point. Camille couldn't stand to hear it from him because he seemed to enjoy crushing her hopes. She figured he picked up that nasty trait from patrolling the mean streets of Los Angeles. Regardless of what anyone thought, she continued to see the family man. She felt strongly that they could work through the inconvenience.

Camille and Ted spent a good deal of time talking about his problems. The man was deathly afraid of his future. In four months, he was going to have to somehow provide support for his growing family financially and morally for the rest of his life. Among other things, he was extremely fearful of change. Often he would speak of a desire to change jobs. He wanted to go back to school and get his degree. Those two goals were certainly something Camille was capable of helping him achieve.

Ted made a decent wage working as an electrician for a small electronics company but he didn't receive any benefits. Being the considerate person she was, Camille asked her mother to check the job listings at the post office for open positions. As requested, her mother came through. Mom tracked down an opening for a position with benefits that required a background in electronics. Camille's mother kindly brought the application home. In turn, she took it over to Ted's house where he left it on the living room table untouched for months. By the time he decided to look at it, the position was no longer open.

Also during this time, Camille was getting ready to enhance her marketability by taking a sign language class at a local junior college. Camille thought this would be the perfect opportunity for Ted to be indoctrinated into the college life. Ted's first day of class was his last. His reason for not returning to class was because he didn't like the teacher. In Camille's opinion, the fast paced atmosphere and the tough curriculum intimidated him. She was pretty sure the weight of his personal problems had a lot to do with it also.

Ted probably felt a little guilty not being around his wife in her time of need. His wife would frequently phone him. She'd try to get Ted to come over and do little errands for her. Camille figured she demanded so much of his time because she couldn't bear the stress of being pregnant and alone. The two had been together off and on for fourteen years. They were understandably dependent on one another for support. Which of course meant they weren't anything without the other. Deep down inside, Ted was not a happy person. Whenever he was unhappy, Camille became unhappy. That became all the time. Camille knew there wasn't anything she could say to ease his tension but she tried anyway.

"I know you're going through a lot right now. It's hard getting out of a relationship that's not right for you especially when you really love that person. I once dated this guy named Tyrell. . ."

Camille figured if he knew she had also experienced some heartache in her life and then saw how she persevered, he could gain strength from her. The underlying moral of the story was: Camille was just as screwed up, if not more so than Ted.

Against her better judgment, Camille allowed Ted's caring personality to cloud the reality of what was really going on. The more she assessed the relationship, the more she realized their exciting weekend excursions were acting as a mask. They were hiding from their fears and issues. Everything appeared fine while they vacationed and played in parks. As soon as they left for the real world their smiling faces turned stone faced with worry and doubt.

As if things weren't bad enough, Ted's wife's baby was breached. She had to be hospitalized until the birth. Like a good, concerned parent and husband, Ted took a leave of absence from his job to be with his family in their dire time of need. Every day, he would spend at least an hour at the hospital visiting his wife. Then he would spend an additional couple of hours running errands all over town for her and their daughter. Although Camille didn't like it, there was no way she could rightfully object to Ted fulfilling his parental role. After all, this could have been Camille a couple of months ago. Ted should have been there to support his wife, daughter and unborn child. Camille had no one to blame for her unhappiness but herself. She knew the job was dangerous when she took it.

Camille grossly visualized Ted standing by his wife's bed, her stomach all-big, him holding her hand while his daughter wrapped her arms around Daddy's waist saying, "I love you Daddy!" The vision was so gross it actually made Camille want to throw up!

"Hey honey, how about if we go out to dinner tonight," Ted asked Camille.

"That sounds nice. What time?"

"Well, it will have to be early because afterwards, I'm going to go to the hospital. I want to make it there before visiting hours are over," he added.

Camille didn't like it one bit but trying to be the understanding person she thought she was, Camille wasn't going to say anything about it. Her intentions were to just deal with it, like it or not! On the way down to the restaurant, Camille looked over at Ted and became very disenchanted with what she saw. Ted was extremely unappealing, confused and now unattractive to her. It was obvious she had made a big error in her initial judgment. By the time they had arrived at the restaurant, Camille's appetite was totally ruined.

Holding back an angry tear, she said, "Take me home Ted! I don't feel like eating right now!"

Looking bewildered, he responded, "Why, what's wrong?"

"I just don't want to eat." Rolling her eyes in her head, she continued, "Don't worry about me, just go to the hospital and be with your family."

"Why are you acting like this? Why did you have to wait until we got all the way to the restaurant to tell me you didn't want to eat?"

"I don't want to be a fill-in for your time until you have to go play daddy to your wife and child!"

"Forget you Camille! You're screwed up! I see why your ex-boyfriend kicked your ass all the time! You talk too much mess!"

That wasn't fair. Ted had just hit Camille below the belt by bringing up something he knew was a tender spot. That was something she told him in confidence. He wasn't supposed to use it against her in contempt. Only an inconsiderate person could take something painful and then throw it up in someone's face. That was so wrong it made Camille think he could no longer be trusted with her feelings.

A couple of days later, Camille pulled up in front of Ted's apartment. She saw Ted standing out front smiling ecstatically from ear to ear. He looked so bubbly and happy his vibe caused Camille to smile just because he was.

"What could he be so happy about?" she thought.

Eager to find out what was going on, she quickly got out the car and locked the doors. Ted met her with a great big hug and a warm kiss.

"Guess what Camille!" he eagerly shouted.

Matching his energy, Camille too shouted, "What?"

"My wife just had a baby boy! He weighed 7 lbs and 8 oz! Isn't that great?"

Camille didn't say a word. The expression on her face must have said it all. It had to be a sight to see. Ted's words made her think long and hard on whether or not she wanted to be a part of this. For the first time since she'd known him, Ted's happiness had an adverse affect on Camille. She no longer liked him! There wasn't an amusement park ride or a vacation spot in the world fun enough to cause her to deal with this bull.

Camille's silence provoked Ted's hostility. "What's wrong with you Camille? How come you're looking all mad? You're supposed to be my girlfriend, how come you can't share my happiness with me?"

Camille was carrying a lot of pent up anger in her heart, starting from the time she found out he was married. For some reason, she never seemed to let her frustrations vent fully. The birth of Ted's child just popped the cork. The birth itself didn't cause the reaction. She knew it was going to happen. Seeing Ted's eagerness and excitement pissed her off. It suddenly dawned on Camille that she'd always be fourth string to his family. That wasn't for her.

"I know you're happy but I can't share in your enthusiasm," she answered.

"Why in the hell not?"

"Because that's your stuff! That's your family and kids not mine! Why should I be happy? Why don't you just go to the hospital and be with your family and share your happiness with them! I'm sure your wife will be ecstatic to see you're so damn happy!"

Ted's happiness quickly jumped from hostility to rage. Ted grabbed Camille by the shirt collar and shoved her down in the street.

"Screw you Camille! I've put up with your crap too!"

Picking herself up off the ground, Camille continued, "You ain't nothing either! You need to go back to your wife and children! Maybe they will eventually think you're something!"

Ted gave her another shove. Only this time, he put more of his back and legs into it. Camille stumbled backwards and again crashed to the pavement. Again she stood up and again he shoved her. This time it was just forceful enough to move Camille a step backwards. That was all she needed. Camille quickly jumped in her car and zoomed off. Three days later, Ted called Camille to apologize for over reacting.

"I understand why you were so upset. I'm sorry for what I did. It'll never happen again."

Ted offered a plan of reconciliation. As he spoke of making up, the female police officer from a couple of years back popped in Camille's head. "If he hit you once, he'll hit you again!"

"No thanks Ted. I don't want to be involved with you anymore. Pushing me was the best thing you could have done for me. You made me realize I can't deal with your situation. I'm not happy and I deserve better. Good bye Ted."

CONCLUSION

Camille was totally exhausted from all she'd been through in her life. It started with her father then Kelvin, James, Tyrell and finally Ted. Luckily for Camille, she learned that she had choices. She knew she definitely deserved better than what she'd received from former companions.

For some reason or another, if a good relationship became monotonous and old, Camille could rid a good man out of her life with a simple command like, "I don't want to see you anymore. Don't ever call me again." When she met a good man, she was intimidated. Camille felt as if she had nothing to offer.

Whenever Camille met a man who was not good for her, he became her world. Not because she loved him that much but because she didn't love herself enough. By helping him, she became a better person and gained a sense of self worth. By focusing on his needs, Camille's were clouded and not handled. Getting out of a bad relationship was never easy for her. Bad relationships were like the Ever Ready Bunny; they kept going and going. There was nothing she could say nor anything the police could do, without her pressing charges that could extricate an abusive man out of Camille's life.

There would be no more sitting around, getting physically and verbally abused while her man went through whatever problems he had. As a woman, she had to demand her respect. She couldn't be called harsh names and get slapped or pushed around by a man until he found himself. Even though he may apologize later, it still hurt inside and lowered her self-esteem.

Camille realized that if a man were that screwed up then he shouldn't be in a relationship. If there is one thing she's learned, it's women can't help their men unless they want to be helped. Nine out of ten times, the man will resent his mate's efforts to help. The bottom line is: if you're in a relationship and you are in love but you're always feeling hurt then something is wrong!

END

LAW ENFORCEMENT OFFICERS' OPINION ON DOMESTIC VIOLENCE?

Police Officer C. McGary male, 11 years of service

I never get emotionally involved in domestic violence calls. I try to always remain professional and to the point. I figure there isn't anything that I can say to a couple that will end all their problems. I just provide victims as much information as possible and then move on to the next call. It's up to them to use it. It's not my job to persuade a woman to get help. It's like a doctor prescribing medication to a patient, either you take or you don't!

Police Officer D. Hodan, male 8 years of service

I think women are part of the problem. I only have sympathy for those who try to get out of the relationship or those who stay because they are in a no win situation. As a police officer, I can't really help them because after I arrest someone for domestic violence the courts let them go within a few weeks. From there, the cycle continues. Battered women need counselors and social workers not police officers. Domestic violence issues are hard to talk about because everyone is afraid to give the wrong answer.

Police Officer M. Jeffreys, female 9 years of service

Domestic violence can be prevented if women don't stick around. I don't feel a woman is responsible for her first beating. Anything after that is her fault. It doesn't matter which one (male or female) I arrest because they are both to blame. Over the years I've realized that male officers give better service to attractive women.

Police Officer M. Swizter, female 5 years of service

I think it's the man's fault in every case but I have a low tolerance for women who stay in abusive relationships. I know that some stay for cultural reasons but they need to adapt. I would like for every victim to take my advice but I can sometimes look into a woman's eyes and tell they won't. If I smell alcohol on the woman's breath then my conversation is short and to the point. I really get pissed off if I find out the victim's children witnessed her beating.

Police Officer P. Andy, female 4 years of service

A man does not have the right to hit a woman! Men who hit women are primitive and they make me sick but as a police officer I have to put my feelings aside. I can easily arrest a women as I would a man. In my opinion, we need tougher laws to protect women because I think women are getting poor service from police officers. I see police officers doing whatever they are required to do and nothing more.

Police Officer J. Loretts, male 2 years of service

I didn't know anything about domestic violence before I became a police officer. I learned about domestic violence in the police academy. In the academy we were taught that it isn't the woman's fault and that officers should be patient with victims. I've lost all of my patients. It didn't take long for me to realize that I can't make an ounce of a difference. It's up to the victims.

Police Officer J. Leek, female 4 years of service

A man should never hit a woman but sometimes female victims make me so angry that I could punch them for their theatrics. I'm referring to the women who make allegations just to get the man out of the house because they are angry. Some try to block the door to prevent the man from leaving and venting their anger elsewhere.

Police Officer M. Roscoe, female 4 years of service

I get really bothered by domestic violence incidents. I become angry with male suspects and sometimes my male partners who think female victims are stupid. Police officers don't understand that men slowly chip away at the victim's self-esteem until it is gone. Most of my male partners wonder, "how can this happen?" I think most victims receive poor advice from police officers.

Police Officer D. Thomas, male 13 years of service

Every domestic violence call is a gamble. Nine out of ten times police officers leave calls and nobody gets seriously hurt. On a rare occasion, someone will get killed because a police officer failed to make an arrest. As a result, the State of California adopted extreme laws to protect battered women. I generally feel sorry for battered women but I do feel they share the blame. I no sympathy for women who get battered a second time and then blame the police. That's like putting on a blindfold, walking out into traffic and then blaming the ambulance for not being there. Victims need counseling not the police. To make matters worse, police officers can get into trouble for giving too much advice.

911 Operator Lacey, female 15 years of service

I take every domestic violence call seriously even though I talk to about fifty victims each day. I always make sure that I dispatch them as a high priority call, which makes police officers upset. Sometimes I give victims advice and I can tell by the tone in their voice that they aren't paying attention. I want to tell them to leave their abusive partner but I can't because I don't know all the facts. It's really frustrating.

Police Officer L. Arcenett, female 11 years

Abusive men make me sick! Some men manipulate woman to their weakest point so they can abuse them. It's really bad if the woman is financially depended upon the abuser. I think women who get battered repeatedly are stupid. I enjoy arresting abusive men not because I feel sorry for the woman but because I want to see the man suffer. I always hope he will get abused by his cell mates.

Sergeant J. Gillett, male 15 years of service

Domestic violence procedures are only in place to protect police officers against lawsuits. Nobody really cares about female victims. The only thing law enforcement cares about is civil law. No police officer wants to lose his job or home for failing to arrest a domestic violence suspect. That's the bottom line on domestic violence!

Police Officer D. Caberro, male 28 years of service

I don't think police officers should be forced to arrest a man for domestic violence if the victim doesn't want him arrested. Victims have a choice. We shouldn't make it for them. Police officers waste a lot of time booking men on the behalf of uncooperative females.

Det. Buckler, male 12 years of service

Every year I interview hundreds of men who are incarcerated for domestic violence. Most of them are shocked they are in jail. They all say, "She pushed my button officer" which I believe. They cry like babies and beg me not to file charges. Many don't commit the same crime again but for some it's a disease, they can't. When they get angry they react without thinking. These men need counseling.

Domestic violence laws now serve many purposes. Detectives are now using domestic violence laws as a tool against gang members. I can't put them away for drive-by shootings so I do it for domestic violence. It's easy to get incriminating information from a gang member's girlfriend after she's been beaten.

Police Officer K. Silvers, female 5 years of service

Domestic violence can happen to anyone. Many of the calls that I've responded to are minor incidents. I think the majority of them can be solved with counseling. Law enforcement does a lot of over kill on domestic violence issues. We arrest people for domestic violence and charge them with felonies. A battery charge is only a misdemeanor.

Police Officer J. Toppie, female 5 months

Sometimes men and women are equally aggressive toward each other. They go at each other every day and then one day the woman decides to call the police. In that case, I know that she is not going to court against him. She just wants us to stop the abuse. I'd have to say we are wasting our time.

911 Operator D. Farris, female 15 years of service

I get irritated when a women calls 911 and says, "My husband hit me and he did it last week too." It makes me wonder what in the hell is going on. Very few victims ask for medical assistance so I have to assume that most of the calls aren't serious. Since I sit behind a console downtown, I can only imagine what's going on.

Sergeant II G. Murdock, male 23 years of service

When I first started, laws regarding domestic violence were vague and left up to the officer's discretion. Few took domestic violence seriously. After several law suits, officers are now without a choice in most circumstances. We have to arrest someone.

Police Officer M. Ramsey, female 12 years

I think parents are to blame for domestic violence. They should teach their children that violence isn't okay. Some learn violence by getting beat while others learn by watching their parents fight. I never saw my parents fight but I never saw them interact in a loving manner either. I grew up thinking that a man couldn't hit you if he loved you. I was wrong! I was shocked when my ex-husband punched me. I suddenly understood how domestic violence victims felt. That's when I started having sympathy for battered women. I think law enforcement does a poor job of educating new officers about domestic violence. Domestic violence victims should teach new recruit classes and not old and bitter police officers.

Police Officer H. Ames, male 4 years of service

Men and women react differently. Women know that men do not like to talk things over but some women still try to make men talk. If a man snaps then it's the woman's fault. Regardless of the reason, a man does not have the right to hit a woman and I feel sorry for victims. Sometimes victims call the police to talk and get it out of their system. Officers have to take each call seriously because they can escalate to a murder in seconds.

Police officer C. Sutter, male 15 years of service

Women are not to blame for domestic violence. Men and women are 100% part of the problem and 100% part of the solution. I never become emotionally involved in domestic violence calls because I've learned that there are three sides to every story; his side, her side, and the truth. Law enforcement's role is very important but I do believe that we can only provide temporary relief.

Facts About Domestic Violence

- Your partner constantly criticizes you and tells you that you are worthless and no one else would want you.

- Your partner won't let you spend time with friends or family. He also denies you use of the phone or prevents you from leaving the house.

- You are always fearful you will do or say something "wrong."

- You believe your "good" behavior will change your partner's abusive behavior.

- Your partner is intimidating and looks for an excuse to have a fight.

- Your partner damages your possessions or injures your pets.

Women of all races and sociological backgrounds are vulnerable to domestic violence. No one is exempt!

DON'T BE AFRAID TO CALL FOR HELP

If you are in danger, please dial 911 or contact your local police immediately. The police can arrest your abuser, help you get an emergency protective order; assist in getting you to a hospital or to a battered women's shelter.

Don't be offended if the responding police officers appear impatient and a little insensitive. Insist a crime report be taken!

Domestic violence calls are one of the most dangerous calls police officers respond to. Police officers are tense during the first few minutes of their contact with a victim. At this time, they are more concerned about their own safety. FBI statistics show that approximately 45% of all officers killed during domestic violence calls are killed before making contact with the suspects. Most officers were shot through windows and doors while interviewing victims.

Do not be discouraged by the officer's initial lack of enthusiasm. Make their investigation easier by waiting in a safe location away from your abuser and by remaining out of his sight. Be sure to tell them where he is, if anyone else is in the house and if there are any weapons in the home. Once the police officers are confident they are clear of danger, they will become more comforting and sympathetic to your problem.

CYCLE OF ABUSE

Abusers often follow a "cycle of abuse." The cycle consists of three main phases: The *Honeymoon Phase,* the *Tension Building Phase,* and the *Acting Out Phase*.

Honeymoon Phase

After abusers commit their abuse, they usually apologize for their actions. Their apology can appear sincere and may include crying and a promise to change. This may be followed by gifts and romancing.

Tension Building Phase

As the Honeymoon Phase ends, tension begins to build. The victim starts to feel as though she has to "walk on pins and needles" to prevent the abuser from getting angry. Sometimes the victim will provoke the abuser so they can hurry up and get to the inevitable and then start the Honeymoon Phase again.

Acting Out Phase

The Acting Out Phase is when the abuse actually takes place. The abuser will yell and become violent. He will do whatever he can to gain power and control over his victim. This cycle may repeat itself for many years until the acting out phase results in death or serious injury.

DEVELOP AN ESCAPE PLAN

If your partner has been abusive in the past or if he has exhibited signs of abuse, then you it would be a good idea for you to develop an escape plan in the event that things get out of control. Women should become familiar with the shelters in their area and have domestic violence hotline phone numbers available. Keep important papers together. Try to put aside emergency money for food, phone calls and transportation in case you need to leave in a hurry. Don't let yourself become isolated from your family and friends. Make every effort to learn your legal rights!

CHILDREN AND DOMESTIC VIOLENCE

For a child, witnessing abuse can be a very traumatic experience. Studies show that approximately three million children between the ages of three to seventeen are exposed to domestic abuse in the form of fighting, hearing threats, observing torn clothing and objects being thrown. Children can sense tension in the home and are affected by their mother's fear and pain. Children suffer emotionally because they are not able to stop or prevent the violence. This can cause a child to experience fear, guilt, sleep disturbances, sadness, and depression.

Children who witness domestic violence often suffer the same affects as victims of child abuse. They develop stomach and/or headaches, loss of concentration and bedwetting. These children sometimes suffer from delayed speech and cognitive skills, increased aggression or they may become withdrawn.

Children can remain safe by staying out of the dispute and refraining from stopping the fight. Children should be taught to go to a safe place away from the fighting. They should go to another room or a neighbor's home. The importance of dialing 911 should be stressed.

TEEN DATING

Millions of teenage women are abused each year by their dating partners. Teenagers are under an enormous amount of pressure to date and become sexually active. Peer pressure among teenage males often causes them to become overly aggressive in relationships. Abusive behavior is often romanticized by male teens. Jealousy and possessiveness may be interpreted as signs of love and devotion.

The situation becomes more difficult if the abuser and the victim attend the same school. The victim is unable to hide from the abuser. The situation gets even more difficult if the couple is gay or lesbian. Getting help may mean disclosing a relationship which is hidden. Many of the abusers are older men in their twenties. Older men have greater resources and power to control younger girls.

WHY DO WOMEN STAY?

"Why don't they just leave?" There are many reasons why women stay in abusive relationships. Fear is probably the most common reason. Battered women often feel leaving will put themselves and their children in harm. They also fear they will loose custody of their children because they will not be able to support them financially on one income. Battered women also fear criticism by family and friends for not making the relationship work.

Although fear is a big reason why women stay, hope may be an even bigger reason. Battered women often feel they can change their abusive partner with a little love and understanding.

POST-TRAUMATIC STRESS DISORDER

Post-Traumatic Stress Disorder is when a victim has uncontrollable emotional reactions stemming from a life threatening event. These reactions include nightmares, feelings of fear and anxiety and difficulty concentrating. These symptoms are common and often lead to insecurity issues in future relationships.

MENTAL HEALTH

Some researchers have found a correlation between domestic violence victims and women who suffer from mental disorders. A large number of women who receive treatment for mental disorders also have a history of domestic violence. Domestic violence coupled with the added stress of sexism, racism, social class and other forms of stress can have a devastating effect on a women's well-being. The combination of stress and distress can cause a woman to subconsciously alter her behavior to forget her pain.

Women can begin their healing process by not blaming themselves for their abusive experience. They should not feel ashamed, embarrassed or inadequate. In order to overcome any form of stress or distress, a person has to first deal with their initial victimization. Victims should join support groups that will help them recognize the root of their distress. From there, they can develop a plan and work towards eliminating the external causes of distress.

LETHAL FORCE

Sometimes men will yell and throw things out of anger. How does a woman know when he is likely to kill his partner? Does he say, "I can't live without you?" If so, beware! Obsession along with alcohol and drug usage is a common factor in homicides involving mates or former dating partners. Extreme depression is another sign to look for. During this time, men may fantasize about killing their victims. Be especially careful if he verbally threatens to kill himself, his partner, children or relatives. Studies show pet mutilation is a common factor in men who kill family members.

MAKING A POLICE REPORT

Police officers are trained professionals but sometimes they write their domestic violence reports generically. "Suspect became upset and punched victim," the end! Each report should be thoroughly investigated to include all the elements of the crime. Ensure the quality of your report by bringing certain points to light.

Point out all injuries no matter how small, visible or not. Internal injuries can be more harmful than surface bruises. Tell the officer if there were any witnesses to the crime like children or neighbors. Points out your clothes are torn or your makeup smeared. Do not leave out the fact that a sexual assault occurred. Be sure to tell the officer you are afraid. Tell the officer if you have a restraining order on file.

INJURIES

The majority of the injuries sustained by women during domestic assaults occur to the women's faces and necks. These injuries occur when their mates punch them in the face and then choke them.

The second area of the body where most injuries occur is the arm. Men often grab their victims forcefully in an attempt to control them. This may cause bruises and scratches.

Other areas commonly injured during domestic incidents are the back of the head, back and buttocks. Once a woman is forced to the ground, her attacker may kick and stomp her in these areas out of anger.

ONE TIME
THE STORY OF A SOUTH CENTRAL LOS ANGELES POLICE OFFICER

An idealistic, middle-class college graduate winds up wearing a badge and pounding the mean streets of South Central Los Angeles. Officer Bentley is an eight year veteran on the force, living and working in one of the toughest neighborhoods in America. Bentley decided to tell his story, fictionalized in "One Time," his candid and sometimes brutal look at the life of a black cop with the LAPD. Bentley says he became a police officer because he wanted to make a difference. To change even one life; he found the only life he changed was his own, losing hope, giving in to episodes of violence and abuse, relishing the power given to him by his badge and his gun. In his novel, Bentley takes on the major issues facing his department, such as racism, sexism and the use and cover-up of excessive force.

AVAILABLE on Amazon.com

Cool Jack Publishing
ISBN 1-890632-007
REFERENCES

US Department of Justice
Office of Justice Programs
Bureau of Justice Statistics

By Ronet Bachman, Ph.D
Bureau of Justice Statistics Statistician

Linda E. Saltzman, Ph. D.
Centers for Disease Control and Prevention, Senior Scientist

Diane Purvin, Children's Services Coordinator, for RESPOND, INC. of Somerville, MA, April 1996

(1) Carlson, B.E. "Children's Observations of Interparental Violence." In A.R. Roberts, Battered Women and Their Families, 99.147-167 Springer 1984

(2) Bureau of Justice Statistics, Report to the Nation on Crime and Justice, 1983.

(3) Walker, Lenore. The Battered Woman Syndrome, p.54, 1984

(4) National Center on Women and Family Law, Inc. The Effects of Woman Abuse on Children: Psychological and Legal Authority, p.6 1994. Also, L. Walker, The Battered Woman Syndrome, p.150

(5) National Center on Women and Family Law, Inc. The Effects of Woman Abuse on children, pp. 5-6

(6) All effects from personal observation and various research cited in Jaffe, Peter G., David A. Wolfe and Susan Kaye Wilson, Children of Bettered Women, Sage 1990.

(7) Various research cited in Jaffe, Peter G. David A. Wolfe and Susan Kaye Wilson, Sage 1990.

(8) National Center on Women and Family Law, The Effects of Woman Abuse on Children, p.7

"Violence. It Can Make You Crazy." Working with battered Women With Additional Emotional Issues by Elizabeth Stone House, Boston MA. 1996

"When Violence Hits Home" Time Magazine Jul 04, 1994

Family Violence-Intervention Strategies
U.S. Department of Health and Human Services
Office Of Development Services
Administration for Children, Youth and Families
Children's Bureau
National Center on Child Abuse and Neglect